Updated 2024

The Ancient Egyptian Metaphysical Architecture

Moustafa Gadalla

The Ancient Egyptian Metaphysical Architecture

by MOUSTAFA GADALLA

CONTENTS

ABOUT THE AUTHOR

Moustafa Gadalla is an Egyptian-American independent Egyp-tologist who was born in Cairo, Egypt in 1944. He holds a Bache-lor of Science degree in civil engineering from Cairo University.

From his early childhood, Gadalla pursued his Ancient Egyptian roots with passion, through continuous study and research. Since 1990, he has dedicated and concentrated all his time to researching and writing.

Gadalla is the author of twenty-two published internationally acclaimed books about the various aspects of the Ancient Egypt-ian history and civilization and its influences worldwide. In addition he operates a multimedia resource center for accurate, educative studies of Ancient Egypt, presented in an engaging, practical, and interesting manner that appeals to the general pub-lic.

He was the Founder of Tehuti Research Foundation which was later incorporated into the multi-lingual Egyptian Wisdom Center (https://www.egyptianwisdomcenter.org) in more than ten languages.The website also includes another ongoing activity; his creation and production of performing arts projects such as the Isis Rises Operetta, Horus The Initiate Operetta; Egyptian Goddesses Operetta; and a few more other productions to follow.

2

PREFACE

Everything that the Ancient Egyptians built/molded/ sculptured was for the purpose of generating energies and/or to embody energies. And just like our electrical system that needs activation by turning on a switch, all Egyptian works also require/required activation by the right actions [sounds, gestures, etc.]. And while these 'stone' marvels appear static because they appear stationary, they are no different than [stationary] energy-generating units like our solar panels, that absorb solar energy from the sun and convert it to energy supplies for our earthly human needs.

This book reveals the Ancient Egyptian knowledge of harmonic proportion, sacred geometry, and number mysticism, as manifested in their texts, temples, tombs, art, etc., throughout their known history. It shows how the Egyptians designed their buildings to generate cosmic energy, and the mystical applications of numbers in Egyptian works. The book explains in detail the harmonic proportions of about 20 Ancient Egyptian buildings throughout their recorded history.

It is the aim of this book to provide such an exposition; one which, while based on sound scholarship, will present the issues in language comprehensible to non-specialist readers. Technical terms have been kept to a minimum. These are explained, as non technically as possible, in the glossary. This Expanded Edition of the book is divided into three parts containing a total of 13 chapters, as well as 10 appendices, A through J.

<u>Part I: Architectural Concepts—Function and Form</u> consists of five chapters—1 through 5:

Chapter 1: ***The Architectural Canon*** will cover the deep-rooted Egyptian beliefs of 'As above So below' and its application to Egyptian art and architecture and the existence and adherence to a divine building code, as well as utilizing design and construction plans prior to as well as during the construction stages, which extended over several centuries for large projects.

Chapter 2: ***The Metaphysical Structure of the Universe*** will cover the realms of creation and its correspondence in Man as the image of all creation.

Chapter 3: ***Visitation Sites of The Lower Heavenly Court*** will cover the interactions between earthly living beings and the lower realms of the metaphysical cosmic structure, the significance of landscape architecture in such interactions, and the major types of visitation buildings (both burial and non-burial sites) to facilitate such interactions.

Chapter 4: ***The Sealed Pharaohs' Tombs*** will cover the concept and role of the pharaohs which requires their tombs to be sealed and inaccessible for further communications after their earthly existence, as well as giving samples of some pharaoniac tombs.

Chapter 5: ***Egyptian Temples of the Divine Forces*** will cover the main function of Egyptian temples (being divine generation), the overall conceptual temple layout, the metaphysical funnel conduit design, the generative significance of jointing patterns, outer walls' physical/metaphysical protection, and the organic foundation roots of the Egyptian temple.

Part II: The Physical Manifestation of Metaphysical Concepts consists of five chapters, 6 through 11:

Chapter 6: ***Architectural Constituent Forms of Metaphysical Functions*** will cover the various architectural forms as manifestation of their corresponding functions [both physically and metaphysically] for "false doors", recessed wall panels, columns and pillars, capitals of columns, porticoes, peristyles, colonnade formations at four different locations, obelisks, statuary images, various roof forms (flat, gable, corbelled, arch and vaulted), stylistic architectural details (architrave, cornice, and torus) and stylistic ornamentation and decoration such as starry ceilings, floral, geometric, figurative, or a combination of two or all three, guilloche (misnamed as the Tuscan border), chevron, and scroll patterns.

Chapter 7: ***The Primary Geometrical Shapes/Forms*** will cover the principles and application of sacred geometry of Divine Architecture, the Egyptian sacred cord [tool], a general layout of sample geometric shapes, the sacred circle as the archetype of Creation, squaring the circle, the primary triangles, and the combined square-triangle 3-D pyramids.

Chapter 8: ***The Generative Square Root Rectangles—"Irrational numbers"*** will cover the generative root rectangles as the hypotenuse of right angle triangles, beginning with a square and generating square roots of 2, 3 and 5; the formation of cosmic solids; the generation of the Golden Proportion from the root five rectangle; the construction of whirling square spirals; and example applications of this form of dynamic design to four locations in Ancient Egyptian monuments.

Chapter 9: ***The Arithmetic Generative Progression*** will cover the role of numbers as generators of orderly growth and progression, the Summation Series and the Golden Proportion, and the Cosmic Proportion of the Human Figure.

Chapter 10: ***Combined—Arithmetic and Graphic Harmonic Design of Egyptian Buildings*** will cover combining both the arithmetic and graphic elements into a harmonic design of the parts and the whole of an Egyptian temple that includes: active axes, significant points, the telescopic triangles, and rectangular perimeters in both the horizontal and vertical planes.

Chapter 11: ***Harmonic Analysis of Ancient Egyptian Works*** will cover several examples from Ancient Egypt from all eras and throughout Egypt that show Egyptian applications of the design elements discussed in this book. Examples include temples, tombs, pyramids, shrines, capitals of columns, stelae, pylons, and doorways.

Part III: The Spirited Communications has two chapters—12 and 13:

Chapter 12: ***The Animated Metaphysical Images on Walls*** will cover the metaphysical significance of wall decorations as well as explanations of various depictions.

Chapter 13: ***Human Activities*** will cover the roles of humans in activating, maintaining, and participating in various rituals and festivities as well as deactivating the powers of the temple when temples and the whole of Egypt is under siege.

Appendices has ten appendices, A through J:

Appendix A: ***General Plans of Sample Egyptian Temples*** covers layout plans of several Egyptian temples, with a short description of each.

Appendix B: ***Practical Mathematics in Ancient Egypt*** refers to the four most recognized Ancient Egyptian "mathematical" papyri and the practical mathematical contents within such papyri.

Appendix C: ***Fraction Mysticism*** covers the reasons that, in Egypt, a fraction—any fraction—could only be a fraction of unity and Egyptian tables to deal with "complex' fractions which are similar to modern Logarithmic Tables.

Appendix D: ***Intentional "Irregularities" In Egyptian Works*** covers the religious reasons for what seems to be "irregularities" in the highly-executed Egyptian works.

Appendix E: ***Monument Appropriations Reconsidered*** clarifies what appears to be monument appropriation by one pharaoh, of another.

Appendix F: ***Sample Egyptian Sculpture Works*** covers a very short list of recognizable Egyptian sculptures.

Appendix G: ***Concrete Blocks Various Types*** covers the advanced Egyptian knowledge of concrete mixes and application examples of such knowledge throughout Ancient Egypt.

Appendix H: ***The Masonic Egyptian Roots*** covers the Egyptian roots of the widespread secret fraternal society called 'Free and Accepted Masons' (popularly known as Freemasonry).

Appendix I: ***Egyptian Influence on Modern Architecture*** covers several worldwide examples of such influence.

Appendix J: ***Types and Forms of Mortals' buildings*** will cover types and forms of residential, private, communal and public buildings as associated with its earthly existence's function, as well as highlighting that mortals of all classes—including pharaohs and priestly staff—resided in mud-brick houses.

Moustafa Gadalla

3

STANDARDS AND TERMINOLOGY

---

1. The Ancient Egyptian word neter and its feminine form netert have been wrongly, and possibly intentionally, translated to 'god' and 'goddess' by almost all academicians. Neteru (plural of neter/netert) are the divine principles and functions of the One Supreme God.

2. You may find variations in writing the same Ancient Egyptian term, such as Amen/Amon/Amun or Pir/Per. This is because the vowels you see in translated Egyptian texts are only approximations of sounds which are used by Western Egyptologists to help them pronounce the Ancient Egyptian terms/words.

3. We will be using the most commonly recognized words for the English-speaking people that identify a neter/netert [god, goddess] or a pharaoh or a city, followed by other 'variations' of such a word/term.

It should be noted that the real names of the deities (gods, goddesses) were kept secret so as to guard the cosmic power of the deity. The Neteru were referred to by epithets that describe particular qualities, attributes and/or aspects of their roles. Such applies to all common terms such as Isis, Osiris, Amun, Re, Horus, etc.

4. When using the Latin calendar, we will use the following terms:

BCE – Before Common Era. Also noted in other references as BC.

CE – Common Era. Also noted in other references as AD.

5. The term Baladi will be used throughout this book to denote the present silent majority of Egyptians that adhere to the Ancient Egyptian traditions, with a thin exterior layer of Islam. [See *Ancient Egyptian Culture Revealed* by Moustafa Gadalla, for detailed information.]

6. To make it easier for the reader, we will give a "value" to a ratio/proportion between two integer numbers, even though it is not. We will also write angle measurements (in degrees, etc.) to make it easier for "modern education", even though it is inferior to the principles of sacred geometry.

4

MAP OF ANCIENT EGYPT

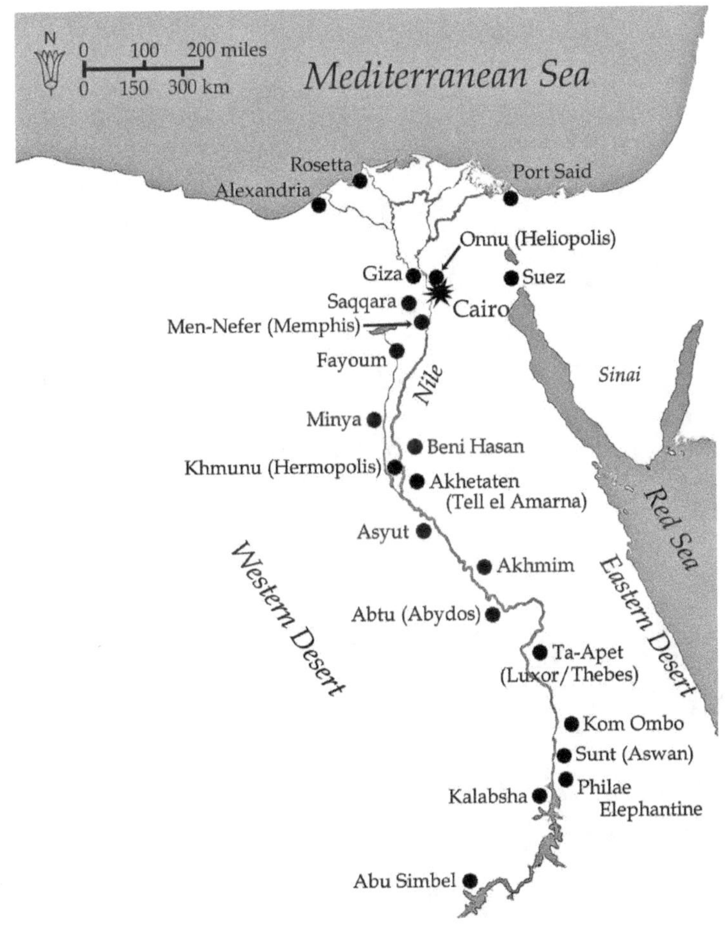

PART I : ARCHITECTURAL CONCEPTS—FUNCTION AND FORM

Chapter 1 : The Architectural Canon

1.1 EGYPT: TEMPLE OF THE COSMOS

Herodotus, the Greek historian wrote in 500 BCE:

> *Now, let me talk more of Egypt for it has a lot of admirable things and what one sees there is superior to any other country.*

The superior Ancient Egyptian monuments are the result of their deep belief and applications of the principal: 'As Above So Below'. This perpetual correlation—cosmic consciousness—was echoed in Asklepius III (25) of the *Hermetic Texts*:

> *...in Egypt all the operations of the powers which rule and work in heaven have been transferred to earth below...it should rather be said that the whole cosmos dwells in [Egypt] as in its sanctuary...*

The scenes of daily activities found inside Egyptian monuments show a strong perpetual correlation between the Earth and heavens. The scenes provide graphical representation of all manner of activities: hunting, fishing, agriculture, law courts, and all kinds of arts and crafts. Portraying these daily activities in the presence of the neteru (gods, goddesses) or with their assistance, signifies their cosmic correspondence.

Therefore, we must forego viewing the Ancient Egyptian monuments as an interplay of forms against a vague historical, archaeological presentation. Instead, we must try to see it as the dwelling place of the cosmos; as the relationship between physical form and metaphysical function.

1.2 PTAH: THE DIVINE ARCHITECT

The Divine energy that manifests itself in the creation cycle is defined by its constituent energy aspects that were called neteru (gods, goddesses) by the Ancient Egyptians.

Creation is the sorting out (giving definition to/bringing order to) of all the chaos (the undifferentiated energy/matter and consciousness) of the primeval state. All of the Ancient Egyptian accounts of creation exhibited this with orderly, well-defined, clearly demarcated stages.

In Ancient Egypt, Ptah is/was the Cosmic Architect, the cosmic shaping force, the giver of form (smith). He is/was the patron of crafts, trades, and the arts. He is/was the coagulating, creative fire.

His role was to give form to the words of Re as spoken by Thoth, according to the Laws of balance and equilibrium (Ma-at). Therefore, Ptah sits enthroned or stands upon a pedestal in the form of the glyph for Ma-at (cosmic law, harmony, equilibrium). [Read more about the creation cycle and its operating energies in *Egyptian Cosmology: the Animated Universe* and *Egyptian Divinities: The All Who Are the One;* both by Moustafa Gadalla.]

1.3 SESHAT: PATRONESS OF BUILDERS

The knowledge manifestation of building activities was attributed to the netert (goddess) Seshat. Her role is well described by numerous titles that ascribe two types of activities to her. She is *the Enumerator: Lady of Writing(s), Head of the House of the Divine Books*, and *Head of the House of Books (Archives)*.

The other aspect of Seshat (and closely related to it) is the one where she is described as the **Lady of Builders**.

Builders, artisans, sculptors, and painters were part of a team that adhered rigidly to the pre-ordained canons of proportion. Their positions can be compared with that of modern designers of printed circuitry or microprocessors, who are constrained within a technological framework of function that depends absolutely upon the laws of electronics.

The Ancient Egyptian knowledge that manifested itself in their monuments was prescribed into technical specifications that were kept in archives throughout the country.

1.4 THE BUILDING CODE

All Egyptian art and architecture, including representations of the human figure, followed a precise canon of proportion. Such a canon was also applied to Egyptian sculptures, friezes, and paintings, and they were carefully planned according to harmonic, geometric, and proportional laws. Plato attested to the remote age of the Ancient Egyptian canon of proportion, and how the executed works of the Ancient Egyptians never changed in character or design over the previous 10,000 years, before his time (428-347 BCE):

> *"That the pictures and statues made ten thousand years ago, are in no one particular better or worse than what they now make."*

Taken in this limited sense, his remark indicates that the Egyptians were always bound by the same regulations, which ensured consistent application throughout its long history.

Plato's statement is consistent with the evidence everywhere in Ancient Egypt, such as:

1. One process peculiar to Egyptian temples is growth by accretion, where successive kings often built additions to the same temple(s). A glance at some of these temples shows that the result is by no means in conflict with the laws of harmony. The added elements are interrelated and grow in scale (width and height) according to a certain rule of proportion, connecting them to the original building. A good example is to be found at the huge complex of the great Karnak Temple. Although it was built over a span of more than 1,500 years, and features 6 pylons, it is still an imposing and homogeneous achievement that produced a harmonious plan of buildings covering about 7,550 ft. (2,300 m) in perimeter.

It is obvious that the overall plan pre-existed and that it was known to those who executed it.

2. Archaeological findings show that these rules were put into writing on rolls of papyrus or leather and carefully kept in special archives in the great Egyptian temples. This is explicitly stated in a number of texts from various periods dealing exclusively with architecture and crafts, such as:

> **a.** A passage from the stele of King Neferhotep (5,000 years ago) at Abydos describes his plan to seek original information from the archives about the exact traditional form of the statue of Osiris:
>
> > *The King spake to the nobles and companions, the scribes of hieroglyphs: "My heart hath desired to see the ancient writings of Atam; open ye for me for a great investigation; let the neter* (god) *know concerning his creation, and the neteru* (gods/goddesses) *concerning their fashioning, their offerings and their oblations... [let] me know the neter* (god) *in his form, that I may fashion him as he was formerly, when they made the [statues] in their council, in order to establish their monuments upon earth.*

The Ancient Egyptian knowledge that manifested itself in their monuments was prescribed into technical specifications that were kept in archives throughout the country. These earliest Egyptian records indicate that the forms of the statues of neteru (gods/goddesses), as well as other artistic and architectural features, had the following characteristics:

- They were well-defined.

- The definitions were transmitted by means of written specifications.

- The specifications were kept in archives.

- The archives existed in all official institutions, such as law courts, public works, cadastres, as well as in temples.

- High officials, as well as Kings, had access to archives.

- The high officials were required to study and implement the specifications.

   b. Amenhotep, son of Hapu, who was an outstanding scholar and the architect for Amenhotep III (1405-1367 BCE), describes his early education:

   > *I was appointed to be an entry-level king's scribe; I was introduced into the divine book, I beheld the excellent things of Thoth; I was equipped with their knowledge; I opened all their [passages]; one took counsel with me on all their matters.*

   c. Queen Hatshepsut, building the temple on Luxor's (Thebes') West Bank, said:

   > *. . . It was according to the ancient plan*

Senmut, the renowned architect of Queen Hatshepsut, wrote:

   > *I was a noble, to whom one harkened; moreover, I had access to all the writings of the nobles; there was nothing that I did not know of that which had happened since the beginning.*

This was not idle talk, for Senmut inscribed on his stele an archaic text that had been out of fashion for a long time. Some of the writings are described as being on leather rolls, such as the records at Karnak during the New Kingdom, or the rolls of the library of the temple at Edfu.

   d. From texts inscribed in the crypts of the temple of Hathor at Dendera, we know that the temple was restored during the Ptolemaic Era, based on an ancient document:

   > *The venerable foundation in Dendara was found in early*

writings, written on a leather roll in the time of the Servants of Horus, at Memphis, in a casket, at the time of the lord of the Two Lands... Pepi.

It is accordingly clear that the project of restoration during the Greco-Roman period was based on drawings dating back to Pepi's reign in the 6th Dynasty (2400 BCE), themselves claimed to be copies of pre-dynastic documents (before 3000 BCE).

1.5 DESIGN AND CONSTRUCTION PLANS

Earlier, we gave the example of the huge complex of the great Karnak Temple which was built over a span of more than 1,500 years, based on a master plan.

The basic features of architects' plans in Ancient Egypt were drawn on papyri. Only a few examples have survived. There are a number of architectural sketches that were executed on limestone fragments.

Ancient Egyptian records found from after the 5th Dynasty were set out upon a grid of squares (equivalent to our graph paper) that made it easier to determine the precise proportions. As such, the vertical (or horizontal) proportions can be read in terms of the number of squares (or fractions thereof) in the grid.

About 100 such grids are preserved; some dating from the Old Kingdom [2575–2150 BCE].

Egyptian architecture was like our modern concept of a design-built system. It was a practical application, and the architect was the master builder.

The basic features of architects' plans in Ancient Egypt were drawn on papyri. Only a few examples have survived.

There are a number of architectural sketches that were executed on limestone fragments.

An axis or a series of axes were the beginning point(s) in such construction drawings.

An axis is an imaginary and ideal line about which a moving body revolves. In geometry, an axis is equally imaginary—a line without thickness.

The Egyptian temple was regarded as an organic, living unity. It is in constant motion. Its intricate alignments and its multiple asymmetries make it oscillate about its axes.

This movement takes place within a rhythm given by the "module" or the particular coefficient of the thing or idea to be defined.

The axis line can be found in a few recovered architectural drawings or sketches on papyri and tablets from various periods. They were, presumably, workmen's notations, and in spite of their practical purpose, they still feature the axis line drawn in the same conventional way as in modern drawings. Two examples of axes defined on ancient Egyptian drawings are shown below.

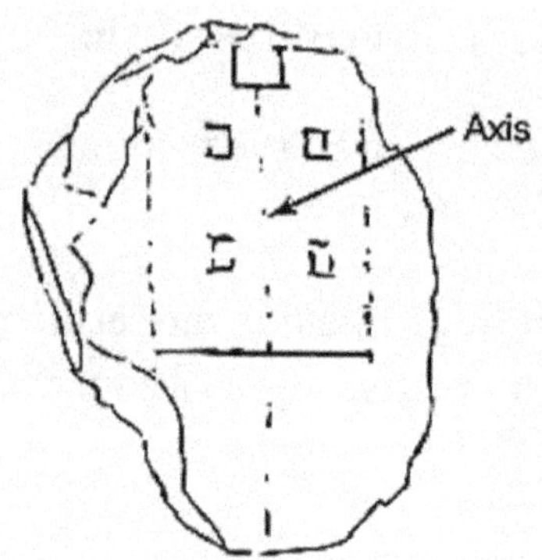

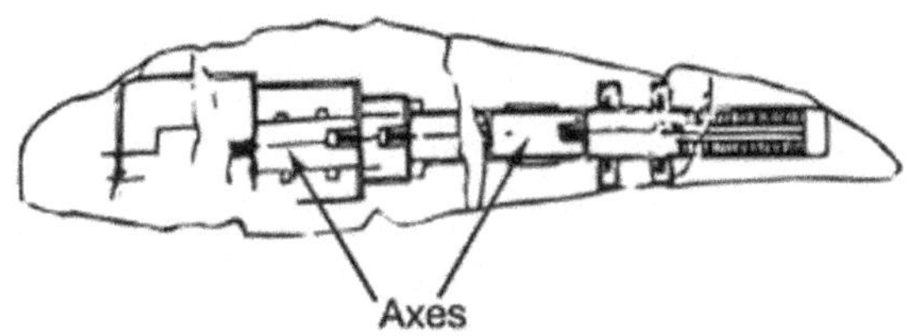

In the buildings themselves, the axis is marked by an engraved line on the stones of the upper course of a foundation slab, such as the case at Luxor Temple.

Samples of such drawings and sketches are:

1. A papyrus that was found in Zoser's Pyramid Complex (3rd Dynasty) at Saqqara. The papyrus shows the definition of the curve of a roof by a system of coordinates. The vertical lines are shown placed at equal distances from one another, and the numbers indicating their length from an unmarked horizontal level define the coordinates of a number of points on the curve.

This is proof that the Egyptians had a very exact idea of graphic representation at least 5,000 years ago.

2. The papyrus in the Museum at Turin contains a projected design for the tomb of Ramses IV[shown below]. There are differences in proportion between the design and the tomb as we know it today which indicates that the design was created prior to the excavation of the tomb and confirms that it represents a project and not a survey.

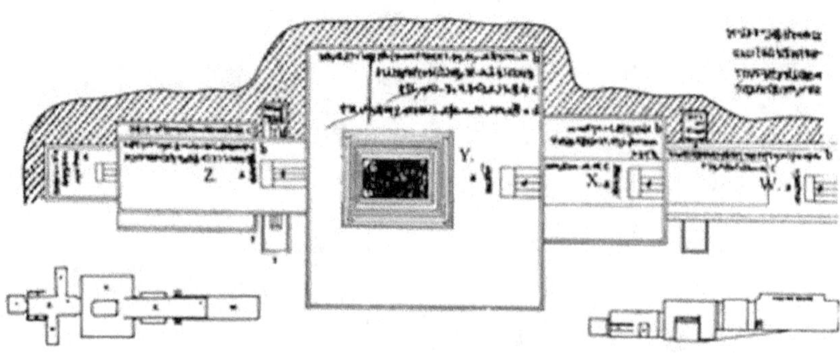

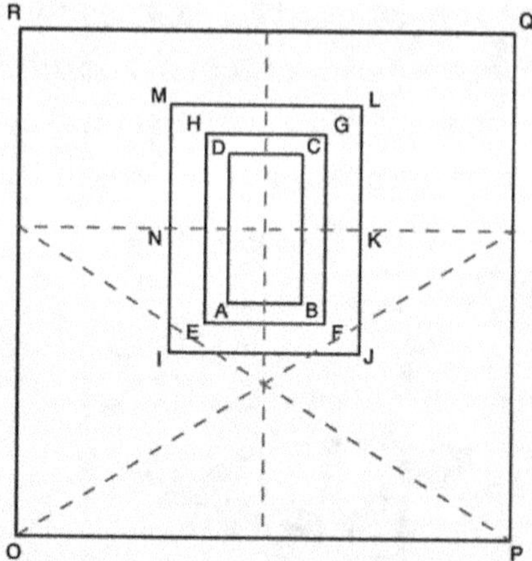

The plan shows, among other things, the contours of the excavation, indicated by double strokes. The dimensions of each room (length, width and height) are shown clearly. Details (such as doors) are sketched on the plan in reduced elevation. It is quite likely that this general plan was complimented by more detailed working diagrams, which is also the case in present-day construction projects.

3. The recovered design plan for the tomb of King Ramses

IV (1163–1156 BCE) in the Valley of Kings at Luxor (Thebes) is shown in a later chapter of this book.

4. A limestone fragment, more than 30″ (76 cm) long. This project for the tomb of Ramses IX is very similar to that shown on the Turin Papyrus.

5. A papyrus with a grid, dating from the New Kingdom, shows a remarkable design for a shrine. It shows that the Egyptians knew how to represent an object from several angles. The two elevations reveal a number of interior features, as in a transparency, and also display the parts of sections. It shows how exact these designs could be.

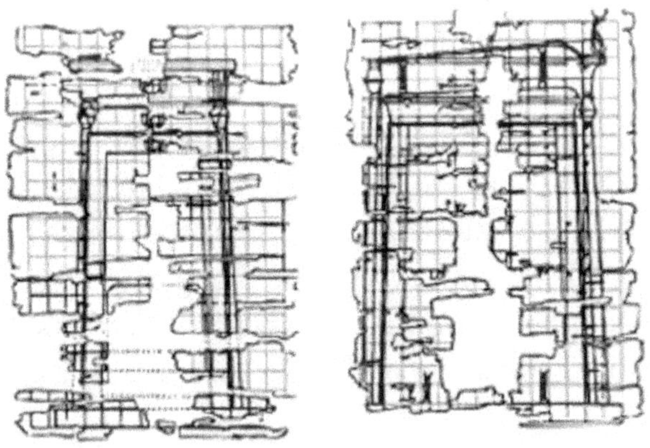

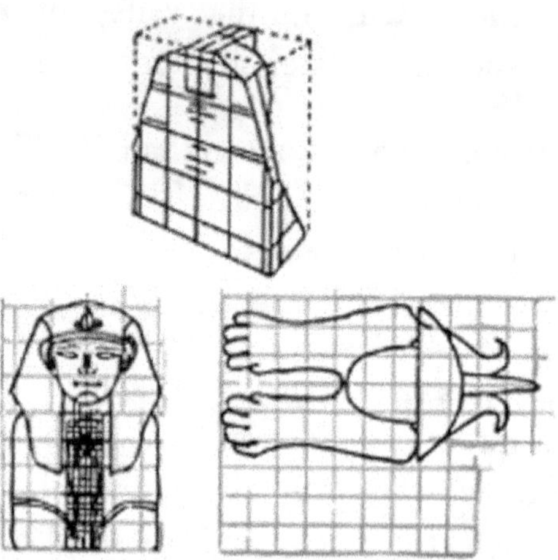

6. There are some drawings with squared grids of the front and side elevations of naoi, capitals, and statues identical to those used for drawings of figures and scenes. Squared grids were also used on walls or on blocks that were to be carved into statues. Human figures, animals, sphinxes, and even capitals and naoi were designed, copied, or enlarged from books of models by means of grids. Squaring on a grid was often used for wall decorations. Remains of such grids can still frequently be seen on the walls of tombs and temples.

Other examples of such design and construction plans will be described throughout the text of this book.

>> Several color photographs in support of the text of this subchapter are to be found in the digital edition of this book as published in PDF and E-book formats.

Chapter 2 : The Metaphysical Structure of the Universe

2.1 THE ENERGY REALMS OF THE UNIVERSE

The Ancient and Baladi Egyptians made/make no distinction between a metaphysical state of being and one with a material body. Such a distinction is a mental illusion, as accepted now in scientific circles since Einstein's relativity theory, that matter is a form of energy.

Since Einstein's relativity theory, it has been known and accepted that matter is a form of energy—a coagulation or condensation of energy. Energy is made up of molecules rotating or vibrating at various rates of speed. In the "physical" world, molecules rotate at a very slow and constant rate of speed. That is why things appear to be solid, to our earthly senses. The slower the speed, the more dense or solid the thing. In the metaphysical (spirit) world, the molecules vibrate in a much faster, or ethereal, dimension where things are freer and less dense.

In this light, the universe is basically a hierarchy of energies at different orders of density. Our senses have some access to the densest form of energy, which is matter. The hierarchy of energies is interrelated, and each level is sustained by the level below it. This hierarchy of energies is set neatly into a vast matrix of deeply interfaced natural laws. It is both physical and metaphysical.

The faster form of energies—these invisible energies in the universe—are called spirits, by many. Spirits/energies are organized at different orders of densities which relate to the different speeds of molecules. These faster (invisible) energies inhabit certain areas, or are associated with particular natural phenomena. Spirits (energies) exist in family-type groups (they are related to each other).

Energies may occupy, at will, a more condensed energy (matter) such as human, animal, plant, or any form. The spirit animates the human body at birth and leaves it at death. Sometimes more than one energy spirit enters a body. We often hear of a person 'not feeling himself/herself', or who is 'temporarily insane', 'possessed', 'beside oneself', or who has multiple personalities. The energies (spirits) have an effect on all of us, to one degree or another.

Since the created universe is orderly, its energy matrix is likewise a well-oiled machine with nine interpenetrating and interacting realms.

Ancient and Baladi Egyptians believe that the universal energy matrix consists of the unity inter-penetrating and interactive nine realms, which are commonly classified as seven heavens (metaphysical realms) and two Earths (physical realms). The number 8 is our physical (earthly) realm. The last realm—number 9—is where our complimentary opposite exists. [For more detailed information about this subject, read *Egyptian Cosmology: the Animated Universe,* by same author.]

2.2 THE TWO HEAVENLY COURTS

The Egyptians distinguished two broad distinctions in the hierarchical metaphysical structure of the seven heavens:

> **A.** At the highest end of this celestial order, there exists three levels in a sort of heavenly court or council that are the

equivalents of the Arch-angels and the Orders of Angels which we find in other systems of religion. Those are not involved with human activities on Earth.

B. The Egyptians distinguished four lower groups that occupy positions in the celestial hierarchy identical with those of some Oriental Christian systems, the prophets, apostles, martyrs, and many great saints. Those lived on Earth for one time or another, and after their earthly departure, they continue to be involved with human activities on Earth.

In all periods of Egyptian history, a class of beings was recognized; some of whom are male and some female. These had many forms and shapes, and could appear on Earth as men, women, animals, birds, reptiles, trees, plants, etc. They were stronger and more intelligent than men, but they had passions like men; they were credited with possessing some divine powers or characteristics, and yet they could suffer sickness and die.

[More info about the interaction between beings/energies in the universe is found in *Egyptian Cosmology: the Animated Universe* by same author.]

2.3 THE NINE COMPONENTS OF MAN

For the Egyptians, man being a universal replica consists likewise of nine components—two related to the earthly existence and seven related to metaphysical existence.

The whole man consists of:

1. A natural body—Khat

   Khat means corruptible—subject to decay

2. A Spirit-body—Sahu

A metaphysical body that leaves the physical body with proper funerary rights and has the power to travel anywhere lasting and incorruptible

Sahu is shown as a mummy lying on a bier, indicating a spirit body that is lasting and incorruptible

3. A heart—Ab

The heart is the seat of power, consciousness—right and wrong

Horus is called "dweller in hearts" and "lord of hearts"

Ab is reverse for Ba = heart-soul

4. A double—Ka

The Ka is the combination of several intertwined sub-components. It is equated to what we describe as personality. The Ka does not die with the mortal body, although it may break into its many sub-components.

5. A Heart-soul—Ba

Since Ab is the heart, the reverse/compliment is the Ba—the heart-soul.

Ba represents totality of man's physical and psychic capacities

The Ba is immortal. When the ba departs, the body dies. The ba is represented as a human-headed bird, as the divine aspect of the terrestrial.

6. A shadow—Khaibet

The khaibit seems to correspond with our notion of the ghost.

Khai = companion/brother

7. A Spirit-soul—Khu

The Khu is a higher spiritual element. It is a shining and luminous component. Khu-s are also heavenly beings living with the neteru (gods, goddesses). Each Khu may then be equivalent to the guardian angel.

8. A name—Ren

Ren as a "name" is the essence of an individual which distinguishes one person from another. When your name is called, you return to the Source.

9. A vital force—Sekhem

Sekhem is the vital power

Re is called The Great Sekhem

The relationships and dynamics between the various components are beyond the scope of this book and can be found in *Egyptian Cosmology: The Animated Universe* and *Egyptian Mystics: Seekers of The Way*, both by Moustafa Gadalla.

Throughout this book, we will be referencing two components/realms being the Ka [the astral body] and Ba [the ethereal body], which are needed to understand related architectural and artistic features.

Chapter 3 : Visitation Sites of The Lower Heavenly Court

3.1 THE LOWER HEAVENLY COURT

As mentioned earlier, in addition to 'The Upper Heavenly Court', there was (and continues to be) a 'Lower Heavenly Court' of several lower orders of the celestial hierarchy, which the Egyptians have distinguished. The occupants of such lower heavenly court are those who lived on Earth at one time or another, and after their earthly departure, continue to be involved with human activities on Earth.

The same exact distinction found its way in later times to some Oriental Christian systems: those of the prophets, apostles, martyrs, and many great saints.

In all periods of Egyptian history, a class of beings was recognized; some of whom are male and some female. These had many forms and shapes, and could appear on earth as men, women, animals, birds, reptiles, trees, plants, etc. They were stronger and more intelligent than men, but they had passions like men; they were credited with possessing some divine powers or characteristics, and yet they could suffer sickness and die.

Egyptians speak of their deceased as *living*, which shows how definite a belief it is that the soul of the deceased return to their tombs/shrines on the specified days of their weekly and annual visitations.

Just as our lives do not stop at death, so our bodies are not limited by their outer physical forms. We exist on a number of different levels at once, from the most physical to the most spiritual. Indeed, in one sense, there is no difference between physical and spiritual; only the gradations that lie between the two ends of the spectrum.

3.2 THE HEAVENLY HELPERS

We will highlight here the most commonly heavenly helpers as being:

i. Family and close relatives

The most common communications were/are between earthly beings and their ancestor spirits. These spirits serve the needs of individual family members.

ii. Community Patrons—[Ancestral local/regional patrons]

The character of such departed souls as community patrons ["local gods"] covers a broad range, fulfilling the expectation of their descendants in the community at large. They behave like superior human beings with the same passions and the same needs, but also with transcendental power. The city is the "House" of the "Patron".

They have shrines, holy objects and statues. They may appear in the form of stones, trees, animals or human beings. They were/are referred to as "him of Ombos", "him of Edfu", or "her of Bast".

Many show themselves to their followers in the form of some object in which they dwelt. The Egyptians believed that each place was inhabited by a great number of spirits, and that the lesser ones were subject to the chief spirit.

The local/regional patron is visited weekly every Thursday or Friday. In addition, they have their seasonal and annual festivals.

iii. Folk Saints

Walis (folk saints) are the people who succeeded in traveling the spiritual Path, and as a result, have attained union with the Divine. Such unification enables them to perform supernatural acts, influence and predict future events, etc. As a result, they become the intermediaries between earthly living beings and the supernatural, heavenly realms.

After their earthly death, their spiritual force/blessing is thought to increase and to inhere in the persons and particularly the places associated with and chosen by them. A folk saint chooses and conveys the places for his shrines to his family and friends during dreams (possibly awake, also). As a result, a shrine (or more—usually more than two) is set apart for him/her. Such shrines, in most cases, are not their tombs. These shrines dot the Egyptian landscape since its earliest known history.

Ancient and Baladi Egyptians stayed/stay in touch with their folk saints. People from surrounding communities regularly visit them at their shrines. It is a social obligation to visit them, especially on his/her mouled (annual celebration).

In addition to visitations, people may also ask these Walis for personal favors. Vows are made by individuals that if the Wali resolves a personal concern, the vower will donate certain items for charity.

Unlike the Christian saints, Egyptian folk saints are chosen by ordinary people based on performance. Once the people can see that this person does indeed have the ability to influence supernatural forces in order to assist those on Earth, and as a result, fulfills their wishes, then s/he is recognized as a folk saint.

These folk saints are mistakenly called "minor gods" by Western writers. [For more information about folk saints, festivals, etc., read *Egyptian Mystics: Seekers of the Way* by Moustafa Gadalla.]

3.3 THE SPIRITED LANDSCAPE ARCHITECTURE

Landscape architecture was an integral aspect of the metaphysical overall design and objective/function of an Ancient Egyptian building, in addition to its obvious 'physical' benefits.

Trees, as part of the animated universe, act as a convenient medium between the earthly and departed souls. The Egyptian term for sacred grove is *Ginne-na/Guineana*, meaning *the place of ancestor spirits*.

Just as the Christmas tree is important in Christmas traditions, where it mediates between Saint Nick and his followers, so we find likewise in the Egyptian traditions, where every shrine must be located next to a tree.

Offerings of food and drinks are left beneath the tree of the saint.

Such trees also serve as places for contemplation. All types of rituals were conducted next to the Holy Tree.

The tree mediates the resurrection or returning back to life.

In the Isis/Osiris allegory, Osiris was enshrined in a living tree.

If a gin (ancestor) tree—a tree with a spirit living in it—is nearby, people often write notes and attach them to the branches of the tree.

Wise men and women consult departed spirits constantly, and periodically spend several days with them at the spirited grove.

The Egyptians love(d) their gardens, which were always found in private, public, and shared spaces such as courtyards. Several papyri show how the Ancient Egyptians prepared landscaping plans around all types of buildings.

As far back as Egypt's most ancient known past, there were parks and gardens. In a document from Pharaoh Snefru's time [2575–2551 BCE], we read about the design of a beautiful park and how the landscaper:

> *dug a great tank and planted fig-trees and vines. . .In the middle of the garden he made a vineyard, which yielded much wine.*

Landscaping public places was essential in Ancient Egypt. For example, Ramses III [1194–1163 BCE] planted trees and papyrus plants in Luxor (Thebes) [as stated in the *Harris Papyrus*, i. 7,11], and in the new town which he founded in the Delta, he made:

> *great vineyards; walks shaded by all kinds of sweet fruit trees laden with their fruit; a sacred way, splendid with flowers from all countries, with lotus and papyrus, countless as the sand.*

In the same above-mentioned *Harris Papyrus* [i.8,3- 4], the text indicates that flowers and exotic plants were imported from other countries and were planted in parks for the enjoyment of gardening and growing flowers.

The Ancient Egyptians were fond of trees, flowers and raising numerous and rare plants. As such, according to Athenaeus:

> *. . . was the care they bestowed on their culture, that those flowers that elsewhere were only sparingly produced, even in their proper season, grew profusely at all times in Egypt; so that neither roses, nor violets, nor any others, were wanting there, even in the middle of winter.*

Shown below is a partial plan of an Ancient Egyptian temple showing the landscaping on the temple proper [Beni Hassan].

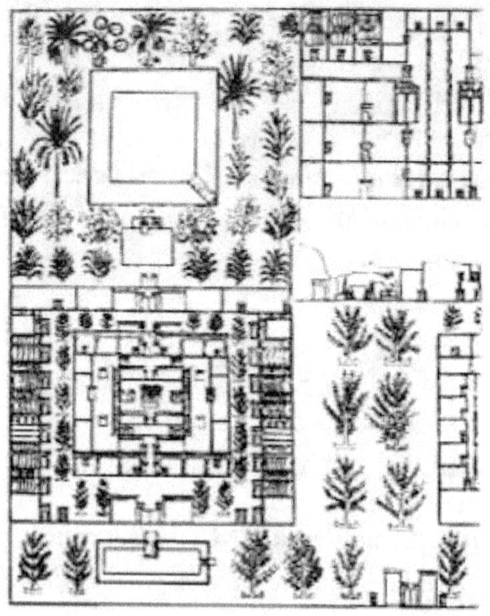

Shown below is a plan for a garden in Ta-Apet(Thebes).

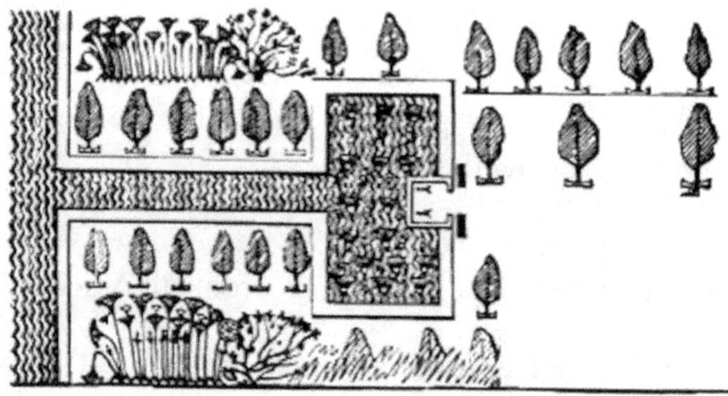

Several remarkable pictures from Luxor (Theban) tombs from the time of the New Kingdom [1550–1070 BCE] give us further details as to the arrangement of the gardens and country houses.

Large gardens were usually divided into different sections, with the main areas dedicated to the orchard (date and sycamore trees) and to the vineyard. The flower and kitchen gardens also occupied a considerable space, laid out in beds; and miniature trees, herbs, and flowers were grown in red earthen pots exactly like our own, arranged in long rows by the walks and borders.

A typical Ancient Egyptian building (as depicted on a found papyrus) had a high-castellated wall surrounding the section. The building is located at the back of the property, surrounded by a double row of palms and high trees. The vineyard is located in the center of the plan. The luxuriant vines with their large purple grapes are trained on trelliswork built up with stone. Through these vine-walks, the path leads straight up to the house. The plan also shows a part of the garden resembling a small park: here there is a fishpond surrounded by palms and shrubs. Two doors lead out of this garden; one into the palm garden which occupies a narrow strip on either side of the property and the other to a "cool tank".

In all cases, whether the orchard stood apart from or was united with the rest of the garden, it was supplied, like the other portions of it, with an abundance of water, preserved in spacious reservoirs on either side of which stood a row of palms or an avenue of shady sycamores.

3.4 COMPOSITE ENTOMBED SHRINES

The composite-type entombed shrines were used, in varying degrees in size, for individual family members of higher stature as well as for 'Grand Ancestors' as the patrons of a community/village/locality.

The design layout must accomplish the intended objective/function/purpose to allow for the return, reunion, and interface between the earthly and departed souls. The prime, most common design features in all visitation structures are:

> 1. the entombment of the deceased [and possibly other members of the family]; with means to facilitate the return of the soul of the departed at specific times/ days/dates.

2. a vertical shaft between the sub- and superstructures to allow the visiting soul access to the earthly living visiting area.

3. a visitation area for the [earthly] livings containing areas for offerings and sacrifice.

4. a chapel in the visitation area containing the threshold [false door—recessed wall/mehrab or even a crack in the wall] where the [earthly] living visitors "meet" the visiting departed soul.

As such, each structure typically consists [as shown below]of:

<u>1. A Subterranean area</u> [called *serdab* by the Egyptians]

The subterranean parts contained the burial chambers, which were hewn out of the rock. The burial chamber was connected to a network of passages and small chambers and used for storing the funerary equipment and for the burials of members of the family.

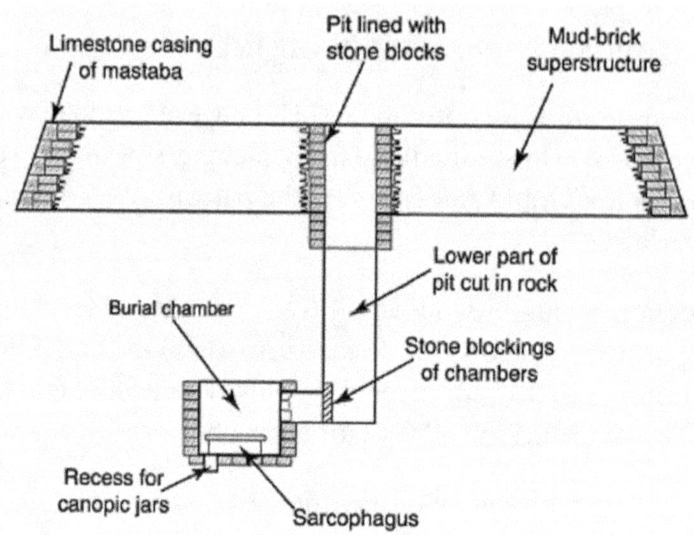

When the tomb is hewn in the mountain, the pit may take the

form of a horizontal or diagonal corridor, or series of corridors, and the burial chamber is hewn at a considerable depth in the bowels of the mountain. In such cases, the chamber for offerings is some distance from the outside of the mountain, and may be approached by going down a corridor or a flight of steps.

2. A vertical shaft—so narrow that it will hardly admit of a hand being passed through it—connects the burial chamber to the superstructure's western wall of the chapel area so as to facilitate the threshold between the physical and metaphysical realms at the 'false door', which was always located at the western end of the chapel.

3. A superstructure that typically consisted of entrance, court(s), corridors, offering rooms, chapel, and sacrificial room.

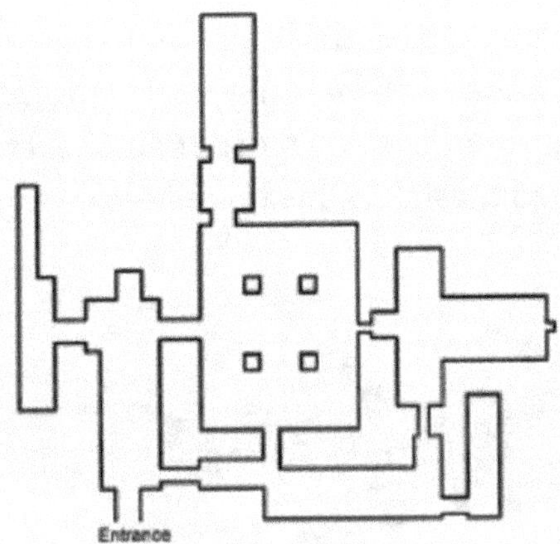

The number of chambers in the building varied from 2-6 chambers, with or without court, and with or without passages.

The public entry faces east and sometimes north or south, but **never west**. The western wall defines the interface between the public and the departed. The smallest tomb in present-day Egypt would have a false door or a hole/crack in the western wall where the living talks to the deceased.

The entry door for the use of the living, sometimes preceded by a portico, was almost always characterized by great simplicity. Over it is a cylindrical tympanum or a smooth flagstone sometimes bearing merely the name of the deceased person, sometimes his titles and descent, and sometimes a prayer for his welfare; and an enumeration of the days during which he wanted his visitations and offerings.

Tomb decoration was not an exercise in *self expression*, but was for magical/religious purposes. The main theme of wall decorations is similar, yet no two tombs are identical. The walls are covered with various scenes of daily life, such as farming, fishing, hunting, sailing, metal-working, music, playing etc. These scenes of daily life have deep symbolic metaphysical meanings.

Since its remote history, each tomb typically **consisted of a rectangular superstructure that was** low in proportion to its length, and had a convex roof. They varied in size from 24 square yards (20 sq. m) to an area of more than ¼ acre. These types of tombs were called mastabas, meaning *benches,* as shown below.

From a distance, these chapels have the appearance of truncated pyramids, varying in size. There are some that measure 30-40' in height, with a facade 160' long and a depth from back to front of some 80', while others attain only a height of some 10' upon a base of 16' square. The walls slope uniformly towards one another and usually have a smooth surface; sometimes, however, their courses are set back one above the other almost like steps.

The outer walls of superstructures were surrounded on all sides with deep recesses.

Mastabas are built of mud-brick or stone blocks. The superstructure is made of dried mud-brick or with a center core of rubble.

<u>4. A chapel</u> in the visitation area containing the threshold [false door] where the [earthly] living visitors "meet' the visiting departed soul.

The chapel is usually small, and is almost lost in the great extent of the building, varying from 14'-4" long by about 3'-3" deep to 10'-4" by 3'-7".

Even today, when we enter one of these decorated chapels, the idea of death scarcely presents itself. Rather, we have the impression of being in some old-world house to which the master may at any moment return. The whole atmosphere is active and festive, with a reception hall in every tomb-chapel. One or two statues of him stand at the end of the room, in constant readiness to undergo the "Opening of the Mouth" and to receive offerings. Should these be accidentally removed, others secreted in a little chamber hidden in the thickness of the masonry are there to fill their places [this is the "serdab" or "passage"].

On the western side of ALL Egyptian temples and tombs there is always a crack in the wall, or what is commonly described as a *false door*. This was for the use of the departed, and it was believed that the ghost entered or left it at will.

False doors acted as interfaces between the divine and human spheres. The false door remained the focal point of the chapel.

The 'false door' was a monolithic limestone with torus molding and cavetto cornice.

The term 'false door' is itself something of a misnomer as, from the Egyptian perspective, these features were fully functional portals by which the spirit of the deceased might leave or enter the inner tomb to receive the offerings presented to them.

It effectively separated the world of living from the dead.

3.5 NON-BURIAL DOMED SHRINES

The shrine for a folk saint is usually a small, square, whitewashed building crowned with a dome-shaped roof that represents the shape of the sky and the Ancient Egyptian symbol for Neb (meaning 'gold'). The dome sits directly over a mostly-empty vault, an oblong monument of stone or brick or wood or copper, usually covered with silk or linen and surrounded by a railing or screen of wood or bronze called *maksoorah*.

While the shrine houses the folk-saint's Ka (a relic of his choice), his spirit—Ba (shown as a bird)—is nearby. The depicted Ancient Egyptian illustration of the tomb/shrine of Hau shows the dome-roofed shrine with a sacred tree next to it.

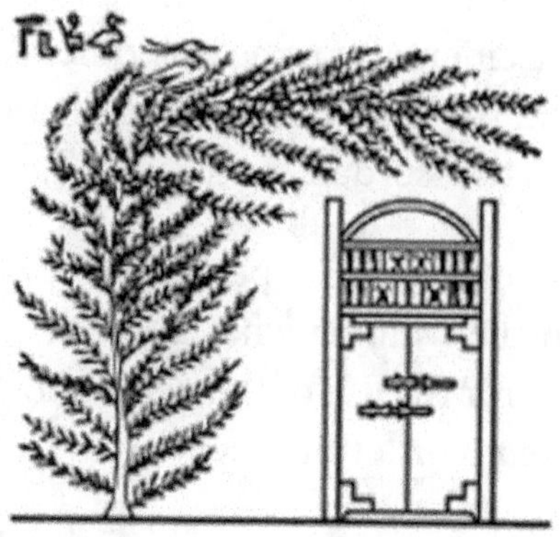

Note the bird depicted on the top of the tree. Over the bird is written **Soul of Osiris**. Everyone, after leaving the earthly realm, is equated to Osiris, and as such, the Ba represents the soul of any deceased person.

Access for the Ba of the folk saint is made available along the western wall of the shrine in the form of a recess in the wall (mehrab).

Chapter 4 : The Sealed Pharaohs Tombs

4.1 THE KING IS DEAD—LONG LIVE THE KING

Tombs for those who were *successful* pharaohs were designed to be permanently inaccessible for further participation in the earthly realm. Upon the death of the pharaoh, the high priest would ask if there was any objection to entombing the pharaoh into his designated tomb. If the public was unsatisfied with his performance, they objected, and subsequently he was denied this special burial. He was buried in a communal grave so as to be reincarnated in another mortal form.

The successful pharaoh will be entombed permanently in his designated inaccessible tomb. The reader may wonder why such "exceptions"? The answer is found on the nature of and role of the pharaoh.

Based on his extensive training with the powers of the supernatural, the Pharaoh's body was believed to be charged with a divine dynamism that communicated itself to everything he touched.

The eternal power of the leader/King never dies. The power is merely transferred from one human body to another human body (medium).

Even the British of today follow, unconsciously, the same belief that eternal power transfers from one human body to another, when they say: *"The king is dead. Long live the king."* [More detailed information about this subject is found in *Egyptian Cosmology: the Animated Universe,* by same author.]

In short, successful pharaohs join/rejoin the highest Council in Heaven which, as discussed earlier, has no contacts on earthly matters. The same Egyptian concept was later adopted by others in the system of Arch-angels.

4.2 THE PHARAOH'S TOMB

These tombs, which were designed to be inaccessible, generally consist of a long, inclined, rock-hewn corridor descending into either an antechamber or a series of sometimes-pillared halls, ending in the burial chamber.

The walls of the tombs are decorated almost exclusively with the afterlife's transformational process from the carnal to the purely spiritual (resurrection) to rejoin the Divine Source. The intent is evident at the burial chamber that shows the end of a celestial cycle. The colorful paintings and reliefs are extracts from the Ancient Egyptian Sacred Texts.

4.3 SAMPLE PHARAOHS TOMBS FROM LUXOR

Here are sample profiles of such tombs, despite the fact that some of these pharaohs were denied entombing because of dissatisfaction of the Egyptian public with their ability to fulfill their duties:

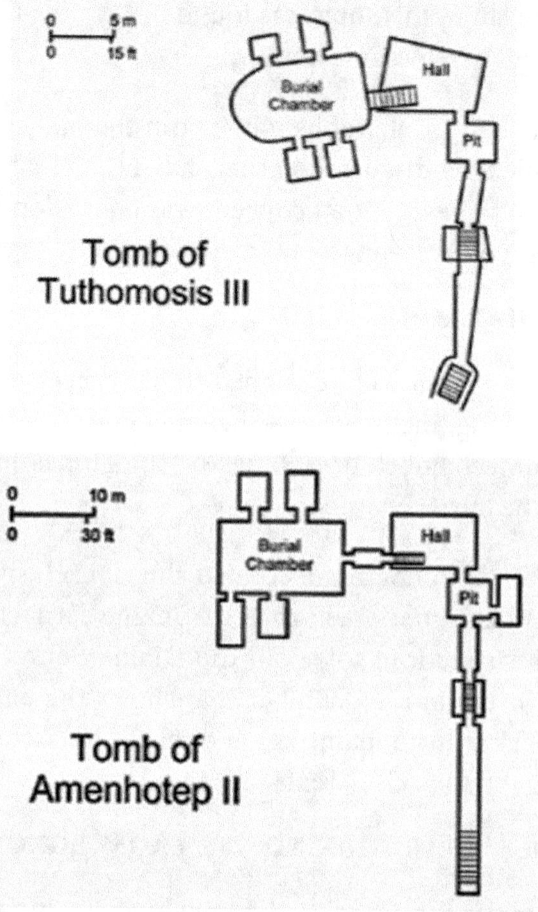

0   5 m
0   15 ft
Burial Chamber
Hall
Pit
Tomb of
Tuthomosis III
0   10 m
0   30 ft
Burial Chamber
Hall
Pit
Tomb of
Amenhotep II

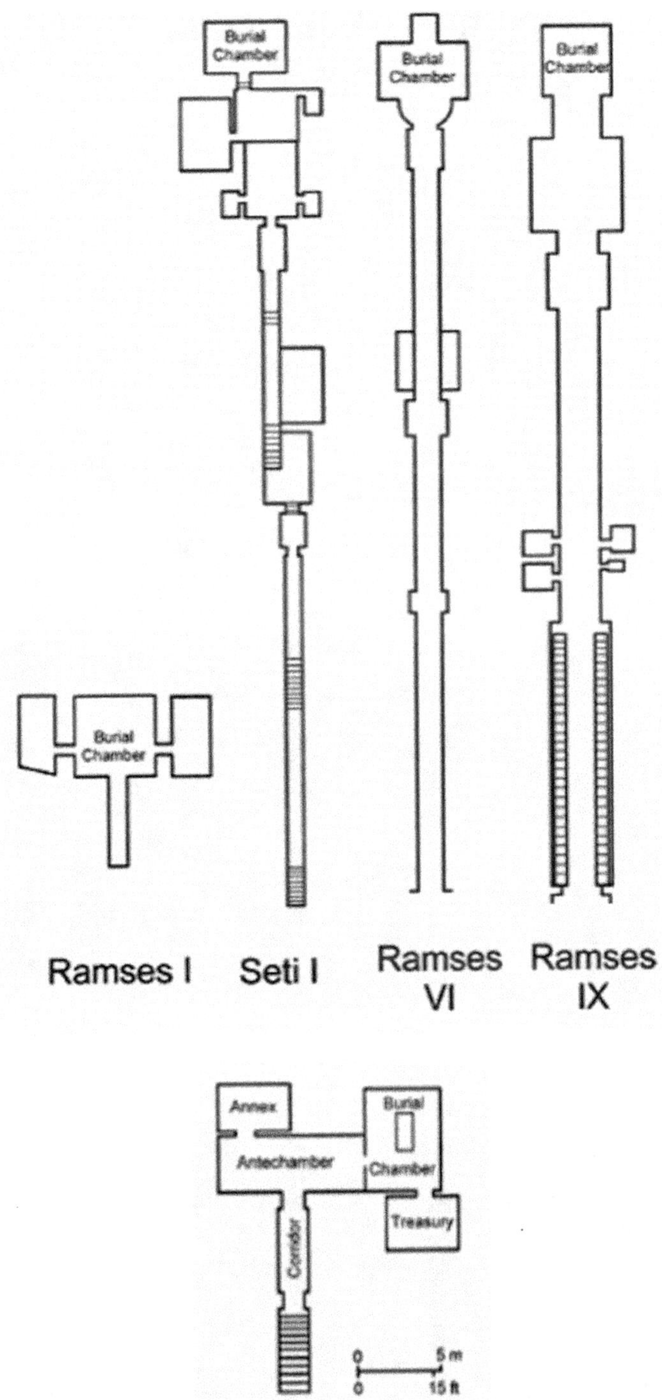

Burial
Chamber
Burial
Chamber
Burial
Chamber
Burial
Chamber
Ramses I
Seti I
Ramses
VI
Ramses
IX
Annex
Burial
Antechamber
Chamber
Corridor
Treasury
0
5 m
0
15 ft

Tomb of Tutankhamen

Chapter 5 : Egyptian Temples of the Divine Forces

5.1 THE FUNCTION/OBJECTIVE OF THE TEMPLE

It is a common tendency to ignore the generative function of the Ancient Egyptian temples. Instead, they are wrongly viewed as merely an art gallery and/or an interplay of forms against a vague historical presentation.

The Egyptian temple was a machine for maintaining and developing divine energy. Therefore, we must forego viewing the temple as an interplay of forms against a vague historical, archaeological presentation. Instead, we must try to see it as the relationship between form and function.

The temple is the link, the proportional mean, between the Macrocosmos (world) and Microcosmos (man). It was a stage upon which meetings were enacted between the neter (god) and the king, as a representative of the people. It was the place in which the cosmic energy, neter (god), came to dwell and radiate its energy to the land and people. As described in various Ancient Egyptian texts, the temple or pylon is:

> *...as the pillars of heaven, [a temple] like the heavens, abiding upon their four pillars ... shining like the horizon of heaven ... a place of rest for the lord of neteru* (gods, goddesses), *made like his throne that is in heaven ...like Re when he rises in the horizon ... like Atam's great house of heaven.*

Only after the Egyptian neteru (gods, goddesses) had examined the temple destined for them did they come and dwell there, as per this Ancient Egyptian text:

> *When the great winged scarab rises from the primordial ocean and sails through the heavens in the guise of Horus . . . he stops in the heaven before this temple and his heart is filled with joy as he look at it. Then he becomes one with his image, in his favorite place . . . he is satisfied with the dwelling that the king has erected for him.*

The harmonious power of the temple plans, the images engraved on the walls, and the forms of worship all led to the same goal; a goal that was both spiritual, as it involved setting superhuman forces in motion; and practical, in that the final awaited result was the maintenance of the country's prosperity.

It is therefore that the Egyptian temple was not a place of public worship in our "modern" understanding. It was the interface between the divine forces and humans. The Egyptian temple served as the theater in which symbolic rituals were performed by the Pharaoh and his designated priests, providing assurances that the society has conformed to its divine obligations of hard work, virtues, justice, harmony, and order. In return, the divine forces [Neteru] gave acceptance, prosperity, etc. In short, the Egyptian temple was the source of power by which all of Egyptian society followed.

These truly divine places were accessible only to the priesthood, who could enter the inner sanctuaries where the sacred rites and ceremonies were performed. In some instances, only the King himself or his authorized substitute had permission to enter.

The general public participated in the many great festivals and celebrations held outside the temples in honor of the various deities. Public participation was a duty by everyone, and an essential aspect in the "worship" process to maintain the universal harmony. [For more info, read *Egyptian Mystics: Seekers of the Way*, by Moustafa Gadalla.]

5.2 COMPONENTS OF THE TEMPLE COMPLEX .

In general, the Egyptian temple was surrounded by a massive wall of mud-brick that was typically set in wavy courses to symbolize primeval waters, representing the first stage of creation.

Outside the walls of the temple were the residences of the priestly staff, workshops, storerooms, and other ancillary structures. They are always made of mud-brick, for they believed that all human beings (including the Pharaoh) were mortals made of clay, and therefore their abodes on Earth must likewise be made of impermanent material—the mud—as shown here in this aerial of the Ramesseum on Luxor West Bank.

Here are close-ups of these mud-brick residences.

Every temple structure was divided into zones of increasing sacredness.

First were the temple approaches and the area within the compound's enclosure—an area open to every Egyptian. The exterior walls of the temple resembled a fortress, so as to defend it against all forms of evil. The temple was entered through two pylons, beyond which lay an open court. This court sometimes had colonnades along the sides and an altar in the middle. These outer courts of the temple proper were accessible to the priests and, on some occasions, to representatives of the populace.

Next, along the temple axis, came the hypostyle, a pillared hall often surrounded by small rooms that were used for the storage of temple equipment and for other secondary functions.

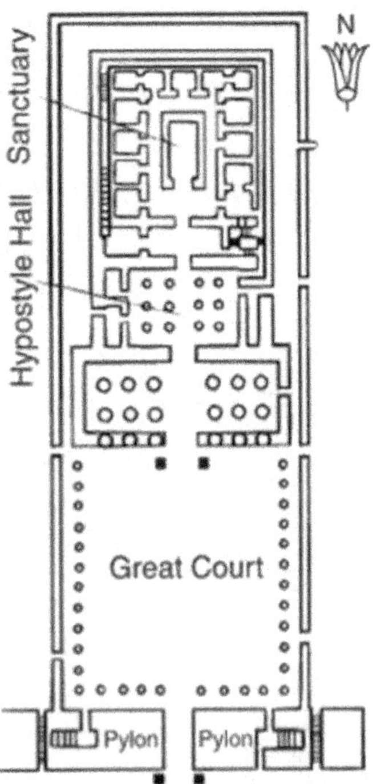

Finally there were the inner halls which only the purified priests were allowed access to, and the sanctuary itself, which could be entered only by the king and certain priests of the highest ranks.

The sanctuary was a dark room containing the shrine where the image of the neter was placed. The sanctuary's doors were shut and sealed all year long, and were open only for the great festivals. The sanctuary was called *the Great Seat*.

Beyond these areas central to every temple's form and role, other ancillary elements were often also present—administrative chambers, residences of the priestly staff, workshops, storerooms, and other ancillary structures, sacred lakes, gardens, schools, libraries, and areas dedicated to numerous other uses.

See the general plans of sample Egyptian temples with short descriptions of each, in Appendix A of this book.

5.3 THE METAPHYSICAL FUNNEL CONDUIT DESIGN

The design of the temple usually started from the sanctuary, which is the focal point. The typical Egyptian temple plan increases in width and height from the sanctuary towards the front. This over-all delimitation was based upon a "telescopic system" of design.

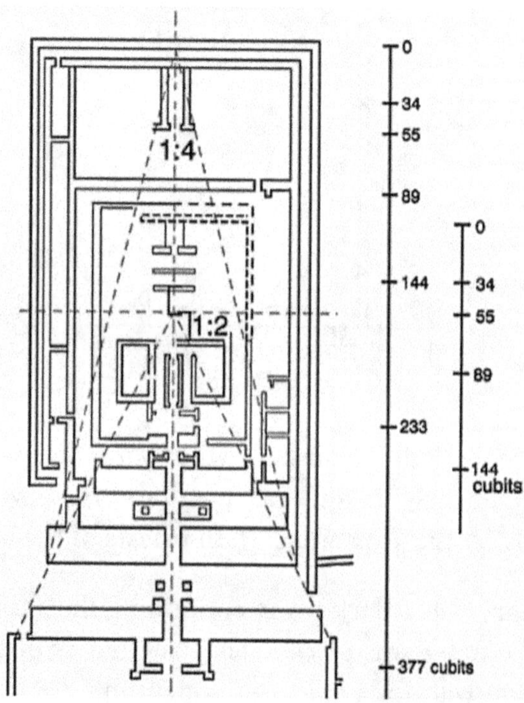

The same telescopic configuration applied to the vertical plan, whereby the floor of the temple descended and the roofs ascended, outwardly, towards the temple's pylons, as shown below in Medinet Habu Temple in Luxor.

In Abydos Temple—the same telescopic design.

In Philae Temple in Aswan:.

The telescopic design allows the flow of energy from human beings towards the seat of the Divine energy in the sanctuary.

Offering processions entering and proceeding towards the focal point of the temple or tomb is a constant theme.

At the end of the Great Court, the Pharaoh or his designates will systematically provide ritualistic offerings to the divine forces as they proceed towards the holy of holiest.

The divine energies will respond to the proper action of man by radiating its divine energies to the benefit of all the worthy.

5.4 THE GENERATIVE SIGNIFICANCE OF JOINTING PATTERNS

In the *Litany of Re,* the cosmic creative force—being Re—is described as:

> *'The One Joined Together—who comes out of his own members".*

This is the perfect definition of the unity of multiplicities as the archetype of the created universe.

In order to ensure the function of a temple, a statue, etc. **as a living organism**, its components must be connected so that the cosmic energy can flow through unimpeded.

It is incorrect to merely think that a connection between two components/parts is only to ensure the structural stability of the part(s) and the whole building.

We can take clues from the human body (the house of the soul) when reviewing the Egyptian temple (the house of cosmic soul/energy/neter).

The human body is connected with muscles, etc., but veins and nerves are not interrupted at the bone joints of the skeleton. The living Ancient Egyptian temple was designed likewise.

The unity of the components of the temple must be like the components of the human body. The walls of a temple consist of blocks and corners, and such components (blocks) must be connected together in a way that allows the flow of divine energy, just like the parts of a human being.

Bas-reliefs of all sizes, as well as the hieroglyphic symbols, span two adjoining blocks with total perfection. The intent is very clear—to bridge over the joint between adjacent blocks next to each other, or on top of each other.

The blocks themselves were joined together in some type of nerve/energy system. A continuation of energy flow required special interlocking patterns.

The practice of joining blocks together prevailed in every Egyptian temple throughout the known history of Ancient Egypt. Here are a few examples of joining applications:

1. Cutting into each block of stone, a superficial, 1 inch (2cm)

deep, dovetail-type notch that linked the stone to
the adjacent stone. These mortices link one block to another—a
kind of nervous or arterial system running throughout the whole
of the temple.

No binding material has ever been found in these shallow dovetail notches. There is no architectural or structural
importance, whatsoever, for such notches, with or without
wooden tenons.

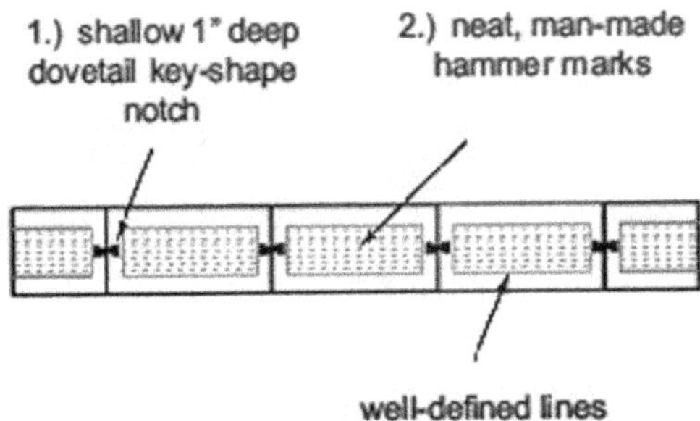

2. There are frequent, intentional, well-defined, rectangular,
neat, man-made hammer marks on top of the blocks.
Again, these have no structural value whatsoever. [See illustration above]

3. Columns made of single, circular blocks have their sections
connected with a well-defined circle of neat hammer
marks. Again, these have no structural value whatsoever. [See
illustration below]

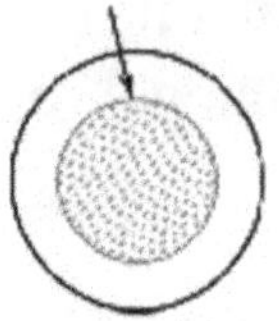

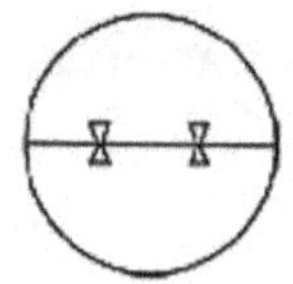

3.) single block column	4.) dual block column

4. Columns built of semi-circular blocks (expressing duality) are found to have a superficial, 1″ (2cm) deep, dovetail-type notch between the two semi-circular blocks. Again, these notches are architecturally and structurally
meaningless.[See illustration above]

5. Paving blocks in and around Ancient Egyptian buildings are set in mosaic style, in order to avoid pointed
corners and continuous crack lines, such as the huge paving blocks around the pyramids of Giza. One can clearly see these very durable, perfectly fitted, square-angled blocks, which are several yards (meters) in length.

Ancient Egyptians, throughout history, avoided the simple abrupt interlocking joints. Creating uninterrupted continuous corners allowed the energies to flow unimpeded. Here are a few examples of joining applications, as found in various locations in Egypt:

1. In the Khafra Pyramid Valley Temple in Giza, near the Sphinx.

Many of the stones are set at different angles. This practice, which was common in Egyptian buildings, has no structural advantage over regular coursing. The additional calculations and labor involved in this type of jointing is considerable, and this Western notion of "design practicalities" or "economic consideration" should never be considered in Ancient Egypt.

The stone corners are not regular, interlocking dovetails, but rather, alternate inverse quoins. The joints go around the corners. To form such corners, the entire face of the stone has been carved away, in some cases dramatically, for over a foot (30 cm) – in other cases, barely creating a return of only an inch (2 cm) or so.

This unique method of creating corners was commonly used throughout Egyptian history. The purpose of the above unique feature is to avoid continuous cracks, so as to maintain the unity of the temple. As a result, the temple's components must be connected so that the cosmic energy can flow throughout, unimpeded.

2. Also found in Saqqara from the Old Kingdom era.

3. Further south into Egypt, at the Karnak Temples Complex, we find the same technique in jointing the blocks and depictions upon them.

4. As we go further south along the River Nile, we come to the Temple at Kom Ombo. Here again, we find hieroglyphic symbols spanning two adjoining blocks with total perfection.

At the end of this particular wall, we encounter the internal organic connections between the blocks of the temple walls. Here we find intentional, well-defined, neat, man-made hammer marks on the side of the blocks. Such work has absolutely no structural value whatsoever (and I say that with full authority, since I am a civil engineer with over 40 years of experience).

There are frequent, intentional, well-defined, rectangular, neat, man-made hammer marks on top of the blocks. Again, these have no structural value whatsoever. This intentional neat hammering is consistent with **an organic, not a structural, purpose.**

At the bottom of this particular temple wall, we encounter other organic design details. Cutting into each block of stone is a superficial 1-inch (2 cm) deep, dovetail-type notch that linked the stone to the adjacent stone. These mortises link one block to another—a kind of nervous or arterial system running throughout the whole of the temple.

More organic dovetail-type notches are found throughout. No binding material has ever been found in these shallow dovetail notches. There is no architectural or structural importance whatsoever for such notches, with or without wooden tenons. We also find frequent, intentional, well-defined, rectangular, neat, man-made hammer marks on top of the blocks. Again, these have no structural value whatsoever.

5. At the Luxor Temple, we find this **organic jointing technique** at the large seated granite statues. An inclined crack in the granite was "repaired" by providing two dovetail-type notches. The symbolic (or better yet, the organic) procedure is inescapable.

6. We find similar types statue jointing in the manheaded sphinxes that extend for 2 miles (3 km) between the Luxor and Karnak Temples.

7. On the impressive paved roadway between the two temples of Luxor and Karnak, we encounter another application of the organic jointing patterns in the paving blocks which are set in mosaic style in order to avoid pointed corners and continuous crack lines, such as the huge paving blocks around the pyramids of Giza. One can clearly see these very durable, perfectly fitted, square-angled blocks which are several yards (meters) in length.

8. Further north in the Giza Plateau, we find the same organic pattern on the causeway from the Khafra Pyramid to its Valley Temple next to the Sphinx.

9. The same patterns in perfectly-fitted huge paving blocks are found around the base of the Khafra Pyramid.

10. The same patterns are all over the Giza Plateau.

Ancient Egyptians, throughout history, avoided simple, abrupt, interlocking joints. Creating uninterrupted continuous corners allowed the energies to flow unimpeded.

5.5 OUTER WALLS PHYSICAL/METAPHYSICAL PROTECTION

In conjunction with the animated, organic, living aspects of the temple, the Egyptian temple was generally surrounded by a massive sun-dried mud-brick wall in a wavy arrangement. This wall isolated the temple from its surroundings which, symbolically, represented the forces of chaos. Metaphorically, the mud resulted from the union of heaven and Earth. The brick wall was therefore typically set in wavy courses to symbolize the primeval waters, representing the first stage of creation.

The Medinet Habu Temple on Luxor's West Bank shows us a clear definition of the whole site. Here are the remains of the mud brick wall at Medinat Habu, even though it is practically in the middle of the desert.

The main temple, as we observe here, had exterior walls that resembled a fortress, so as to defend it against all forms of evil.

Depictions on the outer walls show how it ensures its protection from evil forces so as to maintain its sanctity. The temple was entered through the gateway between the two pylons. There are five main forms of outer wall protection.

1) Foreign enemies being restrained.

2) Thoth and Horus in the act of purifying the person before entering the temple.

3) Catching and detaining bad spirits in the forms of birds, fish, wild animals, and human foreign impurities.

4) Enlightened humans in the form of seated statues.

5) Statues of symbolic protective animals, such as falcons & lionesses.

Falcon of Horus at Edfu Temple:

Lioness at Medinet Habu in Luxor.

The first form is restraining foreign impurities. In Ancient Egyptian temples, tombs, and texts, human vices are depicted as foreigners (the sick body is sick because it is/was invaded by foreign germs). Foreigners are depicted as subdued, arms tightened/tied behind their backs to portray inner self-control. The most vivid example of self-control is the common depiction of the Pharaoh (The Perfected Man) on the outer walls of Ancient Egyptian temples, subduing/controlling foreign enemies – the enemies (impurities) within.

There are absolutely no grounds to identify these symbolic figures as of being of any particular race or region. It is purely a symbolic representation. The same "war" scene is repeated at temples throughout the country, which signifies its symbolism and is not a representation of actual historical events. The "war" scenes symbolize the never-ending battle between Good and Evil.

Many depictions refer to the battle of Kadesh. The famed "Battle of Kadesh" is really the personal drama of the individual royal man (the king in each of us) single-handedly subduing the inner forces of chaos and darkness. Kadesh means holy/sacred. Therefore, the Battle of Kadesh signifies the inner struggle—a holy war within each individual.

The second form is ensuring the purity of the temple entrants. The Egyptian model of mysticism stresses that purity can only be achieved through purifying the heart and practicing pure intent in ordinary daily life.

In the Ancient Egyptian traditions, the active faculties of The Perfect Man were intelligence (which was identified with the heart and personified as Horus—a solar deity) and action (which was identified with the tongue and personified as Thoth—a lunar deity). One thinks with the heart and acts with the tongue, as described on an Ancient Egyptian stele:

> *The Heart thinks all that it wishes, and the Tongue delivers all that it wishes.*

The Ancient Egyptian depiction [shown herein] shows the Perfected Person being purified by the combined action of his heart (Horus) and tongue (Thoth), with water in the form of the ankh and the was, which represents the water. The ankh represents eternal life, and the was represents authority – i.e. total self-control.

The third form of ensuring the purity of the place is catching and detaining evil forces by nets. Netting scenes are a constant theme in Egyptian temples and tombs throughout its history.

Bird catching is equivalent to controlling the forces of chaos. In Mozart's Masonic Opera, The Magic Flute, the free spirit Papageno traps wild birds. This is purely Egyptian symbolism, because for the Ancient Egyptians, each bird (such as the falcon, vulture, stork, phoenix, goose, etc.) symbolized various spiritual qualities. Each species of bird represented a wild spiritual aspect that must be trapped, caged, sometimes tamed, and other times offered to the neteru in sacrifice.

Of special interest is the consistent showing of an adult with his son, wearing the sidelocks of youth and carrying the hoopoe. The scene here is from Abydos, but similar scenes are found in tombs and temples since the Old Kingdom, 4,500 years ago.

In the Islamic mystical poem "Conference of the Birds", the hoopoe is chief of a troop of birds who set out looking for the Simurg or divine principle. In this Sufi allegory, the hoopoe is feminine.

The bird netting scene is predominant since the Old Kingdom Era, as found in numerous tombs in Saqqara.

Hunting and fishing are also equivalent to controlling chaos. The example on the outer walls of the Edfu temple illustrate this concept very clearly, for the net includes fish, birds, wild animals, and "foreign prisoners".

The Fourth forms are seated human statues representing the liberation of the spiritual self from its lower material self. The Egyptian was highly conscious of the box-like structure, which is the model of the Earth or the material world. The form of statuary called the "cube statue" is prevalent since the Middle Kingdom (2040-1783 BCE). The subject was integrated into the cubic form of the stone. In these cube statues, there is a powerful sense of the subject emerging from the confinement of the cube. Its symbolic significance is that the spiritual principle is emerging from the material world. The earthly person is placed unmistakably in material existence. The Divine person is shown sitting squarely on a cube – i.e. mind over matter.

The carving on the seat shows the typical tying of the "two lands" of the two mirror images of Hapi, to signify the ability to understand and unite the dual nature of creation.

The statues of enlightened individuals acted as intermediaries between the people and the deities through proper rituals at specific times.

The fifth form are statues of animals as embodiments of certain divine aspects of the universe.

Mre about animal symbolism in a later chapter of this book.

5.6 THE ORGANIC FOUNDATION ROOTS OF THE TEMPLE

The choice of location and design peculiarities of a temple were not based on economical considerations, but rather on a deeper knowledge of the macro cosmos.

Since the Ancient Egyptian temples are thousands of years old, a restoration/rebuilding (of each) was required every few decades/ centuries. One can find temples which were torn down over and over again. Other temples were never torn down, but were carefully cared for and periodically repaired and added to.

The Egyptians had a rational system in the dismantling and rebuilding processes. Certain blocks from an old temple were placed beneath the columns of a new temple as if it was the seed to nourish a new plant. The Egyptian temple had its natural, organic lifetime, and when the temple had completed its predestined cycle, it was torn down or revised or added to. The redeployment of temple blocks was deliberate, and the purpose of this redeployment was to regenerate the new temple.

Temples throughout Egypt make reference to being originally built much earlier than their "dynastic history". The texts inscribed in the crypts of the temple of Hathor at Dendera clearly state that the temple that was restored during the Ptolemaic Era was based on drawings dating back to King Pepi of the 6th Dynasty (2400 BCE). The drawings themselves are copies of documents that are thousands of years older (the time of *Followers of Horus*). The text reads:

> ***The venerable foundation in Dendera was found in early writings, written on a leather roll in the time of the Servants of Horus (= the kings preceding Mena/Menes), at Memphis, in a casket, at the time of the lord of the Two Lands... Pepi.***

[More detailed and supporting info about physical and historical evidence of Ancient Egyptian antiquities being at least 39,000 years old are to be found in *Ancient Egyptian Culture Revealed* by Moustafa Gadalla.]

PART II : THE PHYSICAL MANIFESTATION OF METAPHYSICAL CONCEPTS

Chapter 6 : Architectural Constituent Forms of Metaphysical Functions

6.1 "FALSE DOORS"—THE PHYSICAL METAPHYSICAL THRESHOLD

On the western side of ALL Egyptian temples, shrines, and private tombs of all eras of the Ancient Egyptian history, there is always a crack in the wall—or what is commonly described as a *false door.*

The west is the point of entry of the departed spirit. It is the threshold between the physical earthly realm and the meta-physical realm.

The "false door" is basically a form of recessed wall with stone sockets similar in details to a regular door/window that is able to open and shut. The "false door" can take the form of *'mehrab'*, a niche in the wall that may contain an effigy or a relic.

In divine temples, the false door is found at the very back of the sanctuary and acts as the interface between the divine and human spheres.

Incoming human action forms and directional flow ends at the false door, and the outflow of divine blessings begins and flows outwardly towards the temple's entry.

Looking, for example, at the massive temple at Medinet Habu on Luxor West bank—and looking at its Western Wall—

we find—the false door:

Further north at Abydos, we find a similar false door on its Western wall.

Likewise, at hundreds of tombs/ mastabas in the Giza plateau:

False doors are also found along the western walls of tombs in Saqqara:

The term 'false door' is itself something of a misnomer, as, from the Egyptian's perspective, these features were fully functional portals by which the spirit of the deceased might leave or enter the inner tomb to receive the offerings presented to them.

Complementary features at false doors in tombs:

1. Most of these panels show the owner in standing or seated poses before a table of offerings. The figure of the owner is carved in a frontal aspect, stepping out over the threshold of the door. The reliefs of the deceased in a standing pose also appear on the jambs of the false door, thus representing the owner coming forth to receive the funerary offerings.

2. A table of offerings in front of the deceased figure is piled with sliced loaves of bread and simple texts enumerating various food and drink offerings which extend in range from the staple bread and beer to beef and fowl, vegetables, clothing, and sacramental oils. The altar, with its slices of bread, may be supplemented by other tables containing offerings or libation vessels.

3. Visitors are bringing the sacrificial animals and birds and

cutting up the sacrificial bull at the door of the tomb. In the middle is the deceased man, seated under his pavilion (signifying a different realm) and receiving the sacrifice.

4. Behind the door is the main burial shaft. The main shaft led from the middle of the roof of the mastaba to the burial chamber.

The Festival Meetings at the "False" Doors

On festivals and days of offering, when the visitors presented the banquet with the customary rites, this great painted figure, in the act of advancing, and seen by the light of flickering torches or smoking lamps, might well appear endowed with life. It was as if the deceased ancestor himself stepped out of the wall and mysteriously stood before his descendants to claim their homage. The inscription on the lintel repeats, once more, the name and rank of the deceased. Faithful portraits of him and of other members of his family figure in the bas-reliefs on the door posts. Scenes depict him seated tranquilly at a table with the details of the feast carefully recorded at his side, from the first moment when water is brought to him for ablution to that when, all culinary skill being exhausted, he has but to return to his dwelling in a state of beatified satisfaction.

By the divine favor, the soul (or rather the doubles [Ka-s] of the bread, meat, and beverages) passed into the other world and there refreshed the human double [Ka]. It was not, however, necessary that the offering should have a material existence in order to be effective. The first comer who should repeat aloud the name and the formulas inscribed upon the stone secured for the unknown occupant, by this means alone, the immediate possession of all the things which he enumerated.

6.2 RECESSED WALLS

The "false doors" were always built with successive recesses and projections

The style of recessed paneling of the 'false door' was also used

extensively in the construction of mastabas (the above-ground superstructure of older tombs).

The earliest known major project utilizing such technique, the enclosure wall of the Zoser Complex at Saqqara, was built several centuries prior to the large pyramids of Egypt. It is a major achievement by itself.

The wall was uncovered by archaeological excavation in 1926. This wall may not look Egyptian only because its neat architecture has been copied in many modern Western cities.

More than a square mile of desert is enclosed within the wall. When complete, the enclosure wall was nearly 600 yards (549 m) long and 300 yards (274 m) wide, and rose to a height of over 30 feet (9.1 m). As such, the enclosure wall was, by itself, an impressive project. Its successive recesses and projections required more than triple the amount of both stone and labor compared to a similar simple wall.

It is built of limestone and faced with finely polished limestone. As such, the enclosure wall was an impressive project.

Many 20th century architects, eager to break free of the Victorian clutter and other demoralized European architectural forms, went back to Egypt for inspiration. Saqqara and the equally clean-lined temple of Hatshepsut at Luxor, particularly, suited emerging contemporary styles.

The commemorative temple built by Queen Hatshepsut is called, in Egyptian, *The Most Splendid of All*. It was a reduplication of an earlier temple built during the Middle Kingdom era. One can see its remains next to the Hatshepsut Temple. Such temple(s) have a similar design to the Enclosure Wall at Saqqara.

Many scholars, architects, and visitors consider this temple the finest in Egypt, and one of the great architectural masterpieces of the world.

Along with Saqqara, this temple has exercised considerable

direct and indirect influence on contemporary architectural thinking all over the world.

6.3 COLUMNS AND PILLARS

There are thousands of columns in Ancient Egyptian buildings. Most of them are in the simplest tomb chapels and mastabas, numbered by the hundreds, and are found over 5,000 years ago. The typical tomb chapel had a portico and a columned room, and columns were an integral part of the structure.

For the Western-minded person, a column is an un-animated vertical support for a beam or a roof. To this mindset, columns may look *pretty*, with pretty column tops and decorations that have a variety of design styles.

The columns in the Egyptian temples were not just supporting structures. Columns, like the rest of the features in the temples, were part of the organic form and function of these sacred places. They were covered with corresponding colored decorative paintings to highlight their organic function.

The Ancient Egyptians' mastery of the vertical principle was manifested, among other things, in the long lines of their lofty pyramidal towers, their obelisks, and the lengthy columns that extended up the whole front of their buildings prior to their existence anywhere else.

The Western mindset, so obsessed with the "evolution" of everything, looks at types of columns as a progression/ evolution from a simple square to a fancy round style.

Yet, the fact of the matter is that even nowadays we see all shapes of columns utilized for various locations and reasons. The same thing was true in Ancient Egypt, where all types were used—and there was no artificial, so-called "evolution".

Throughout the Egyptian monuments we find the manifestation

of the vertical principle being disclosed in all types of supporting columns.

From the advanced design of twin columns to increasing the column design capacity by giving it a lateral [wall] support—as found in Saqqara.

From the simple square in the elegant Hatshepsut Temple

to the polygonal form in the same temple—

and by simply using the multiple flat facets of the polygonal form by hollowing the flat faces into grooves, resulting in a fluted column.

Egyptian Doric columns can be found at the southern buildings, in Saqqara.

Free-standing supporting "Doric" columns are found in the tombs of Beni Hasan in Middle Egypt which are dated to the Middle Kingdom Era, thousands of years before it was found in Greece.

Below are the plan and profiles of one of these tombs of Beni Hasan.

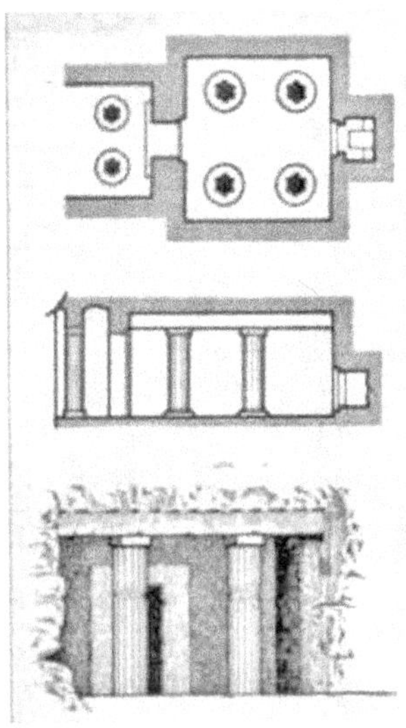

Then we have the simple, round, free-standing supporting columns in the tombs of the Pyramid Age at the Giza Plateau.

And at the glorious hypostyle hall at the Karnak Temples in Luxor:

And then we have the most sophisticated columns, with convex, reeded cross-sections.

- Some had the same width/diameter.

- Others with variable width/diameter.

In summary, pillars/columns in Ancient Egypt, as well as our 'modern times', may be:

– Free-standing or engaged.

– Supporting (weight bearing) or carrying no bearing weight

– Interior or exterior (facade). Just like today, walls could be used between them to enclose an area.

– Columns could act

– individually or
– in twin-form, or with a partial wall, so as to reduce their effective lateral length

Columns in Egypt varied in size from the huge to elegant slender Egyptian columns known as reeded columns.

Columns in Egypt can be categorized according to two main variables:

A. Cross-Section

1. Square – which was also the basic shape of all other different shapes.
2. Polygonal – created from a square
3. Fluted (concave) – created from a polygonal
4. Simple Round – created from a square
5. Reeded/Bunch (convex) – created from a square

B. Vertical Configuration

1. Same width/diameter throughout the length of the column
2. Variable width/diameter throughout the length of the column

The Egyptian column was constructed of several pieces; but it consisted of half (not of whole) drums, with the joint placed alternately one way and the other; each two at right angles with those next to, below, and above them.

A-1. The Square Pillar

Square pillars are found in the earliest constructed porticoes and in the peristyles of the old temples. Practically all tomb chapels since pre-dynastic times had a typical pillared rooms with such square pillars.

Square-shaped pillars were utilized sometimes in combination with a statue of Osiris. This form is commonly known as a "Osiride pillar". Such a form is found as far back as the times of the Middle Kingdom and consisted of engaged statues of Osiris, usually on the pillars' front surfaces.

The square configuration was the basic shape for the outlines of all other different shapes.

A-2. Polygonal X-Section

The first stage in the formation of the polygonal and circular fluted column is accomplished by cutting off the four corners of a square pillar. The square shape was therefore converted into an octagonal shaft. The resulting eight sides were again subdivided into 12, 16, 20, and 32 sides.

A-3. Fluted (Concave) X-Section

The multiple flat facets of a polygonal cross-section were there- after hollowed into grooves, resulting in a **rounded, fluted cross-section**. The Egyptian fluted **Doric shafts** can be found at the southern buildings in Saqqara.

There is no doubt that the Egyptians were fashioning Doric columns 2,000 years before the Greeks, as evident throughout Egypt and as found, for example, in Saqqara's Zoser Complex, at both the 'southern' and 'northern' buildings. Just beyond the Heb-set Court lie the Southern Buildings (distinguished from the set of buildings just beyond them, known as the Northern Buildings).

The Northern Building, with its **fluted/Doric** columns, is similar to its southern counterpart except that the columns are shaped like stalks of an open blossom and carved on the façade. These reproduce an opened stalk with extreme fidelity and beauty, even to the point of reproducing in stone the softened triangle of the actual stalk and the thickening of the stem above the ground line before it tapers delicately to the bud in flower.

In addition to the fluted Doric columns of 4,500 years ago in Saqqara, we find them used in other places throughout Egypt, such as the Middle Kingdom era's tombs of Beni Hassan, as evident in the columns at the outer court of Khnumhotep tomb (#3).

Those at Beni Hassan are 3'-4' in diameter, and 16' 8.5" high. They are carved with 16 elegant faces or grooves along its shaft. These **fluted columns**, along with the capitals and abacus, are exactly the same as the popularly-announced **Doric** Order of Greece, preceding it by at least 1,500 years.

The wrongly-called *Greek Doric* columns were actually fashioned in Egypt at least two thousand years before they were copied by the Greeks. It was doubtless from this and other old monuments throughout Egypt that the Greeks borrowed their Doric shaft.

A-4. Simple round X-Section from square are found in mastabas and tombs in Giza, Saqqara, and elsewhere in Egypt more than 5,000 years ago.

A-5. The Reeded X-Section—convex with same diameter or varying diameter. Beautiful reeded columns are to be found as far back as the Old Kingdom era at Zoser complex. The Ancient

Egyptian reeded columns were an imitation of columns made of bound bunches of reeds.

It should be noted that the 'reeded' x-section is more difficult to form because of its convex style as compared to the concave indentation of the 'Doric' shaft—especially when the reeded-type column varies in width. Reeded-type columns must also be pre-designed, based on knowledge of circle properties and its equal divisions.

The most elegant of the water-plant columns are those in the tombs of Beni Hassan, where they were used contemporaneously with the polygonal and fluted order.

The above were a general characterization of the various shapes and forms. The Egyptian utilized these forms in a wide range, from simple to more stylized applications in varying degrees of stylization from a simple painting to body formations. All such stylizations were consistent with the main objective/function and were intended to enhance and amplify each's function.

6.4 CAPITALS OF COLUMNS

Columns and their capitals, like the rest of the features in the Egyptian temples, were part of the organic form and function of these sacred places.

The Egyptians had two principal types of capitals for their columns:

- **The closed bud,** and
- **The open blossom.**

The closed bud is always found in outer courts and away from the central axis of the inner temple.

The open blossom—wide bell-shaped capitals representing the opened umbel of the plant—is always found in the temple central areas. The blossom signifies the renewal of life.

The open blossom form always relates to renewal (rebirth), as is the case with the neter (god) Nefer-Tum. The Ancient Egyptian texts describe Nefer-Tum as being ***born anew each morning from the lily.***

As far back as 4,400 years ago, we read in the commonly known Pyramid Texts, addressing the Pharaoh Unas:

> ***"Rise like Nefer-Tum from the lily and to come forth on the horizon every day".***

Plant forms symbolize life and regeneration, and the flowering top of the plant/column symbolizes this perpetual renewal/creation.

Also, Egyptians show **numerous stylized forms of each theme** of capital forms, each with its corresponding floral motifs, such as a modified form of the later type being the peculiar inverted campaniform capital of the tent-pole column. These tent-pole-type columns were used in stone as well as in wooden applications to support light structures such as tents, shrines, kiosks or ships' cabins, since the Old Kingdom era. They are also prominently found in the festival hall of Tuthomosis III (1490-1436 BCE) at Karnak.

Another variation of the two principled types is the Egyptian ***Doric* capital**, which is a slight modification of the Egyptian water-plant column.

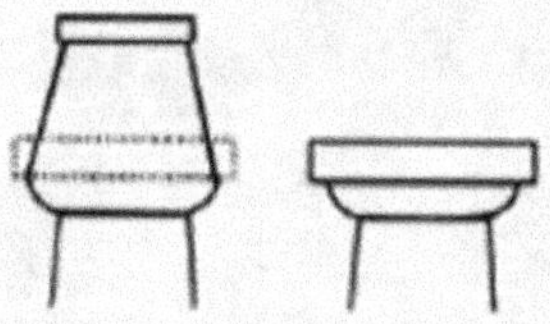

As the illustration shows, once the upper part of the water-plant is removed and the top slab is brought down, the result is the shape of the *Doric capital*.

The **water-plant capital** with the blossom and bud, as well as the palm-tree column, were all in use at least as early as the 6th Dynasty (2323–2150 BCE).

It should also be noted that the circlet around the neck of the early Greek column is very similar to the much older Egyptian bands tied round the cluster of water-plants.

An Abacus is a slab forming the uppermost part of the capital of a column. A capital, resembling a bunch of flax or other flowers, is also represented in early Ancient Egyptian paintings, supporting wooden canopies.

Hathoric/Sistraform Capital

Hathoric columns are found as far back as the Middle Kingdom era and usually consisted of a shaft surmounted by a capital bearing the features of the cow-headed netert (goddess). Sistrum columns are also associated with Hathor, and they represent in their shafts and capitals the handles and rattles of the sistrum—the principle attribute of this netert (goddess).

In temples that relate to Hathor, the Egyptians used the so-called Hathoric/Sistraform capital which are found in temples before the time of the New Kingdom. The upper part of the pillar is adorned, in very low relief, with a face recognizable by the two cow's ears as that of Hathor, in some Egyptian sanctuaries, as a pillar carved in this fashion.

Hathoric/Sistraform capitals can later be seen at several Egyptian temples, such as:

   i. Hatshepsut temple on Luxor's west bank,

   ii. Nefertari temple at Abu Simbel

   iii. Dendara Temple

—-The above is a general characterization of the various shapes and forms. The Egyptian utilized these forms in a wide range from simple applications to more stylized applications in a varying degree of stylization from a simple paintings to body formations. All such stylizations were consistent with the main objective/function and were intended to enhance and amplify each's function.

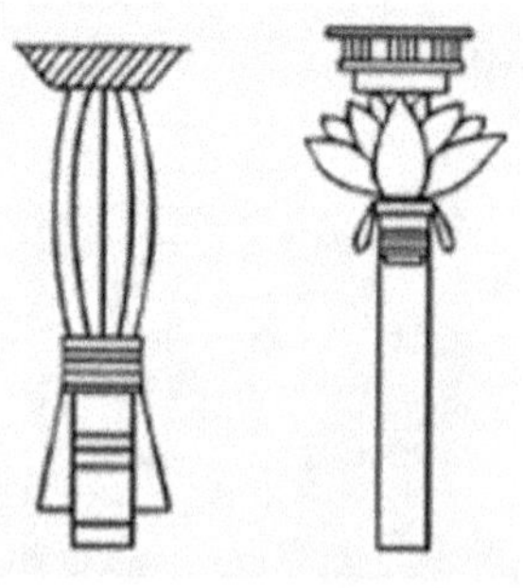

The design of capitals in Ancient Egypt was based on 1:2, 1:4, and 5:8 Neb (Golden) triangles, as shown later in this book.

6.5 PORTICOES AND PERISTYLES

Porticoes and peristyles were used by the Egyptians over 5,000 years ago, and were a constant part of hundreds of tombs. Chapels. and temples throughout Ancient Egypt since its remotest history.

Portico is defined as a porch or covered walk consisting of a roof supported by columns, often at the entrance or across the front of a building. Colonnade has been used in Egypt since its earliest history.

Such an architectural feature was the typical entry form for mastabas, rock-hewn tombs, etc., as shown here in Giza tombs (Old Kingdom Era):

In Beni Hasan (Middle Kingdom Era):

in the New Kingdom Era at the Hatshepsut Temple, which shows square and polygonal shafts in the porticos:

Peristyle is defined as a row of columns forming an enclosure or supporting a roof; or any area or enclosure so formed as a court.

Again, we find such an architectural feature throughout all eras of Ancient Egyptian history and in all Egyptian regions.

6.6 THE ORGANIC COLONNADES

We have addressed columns as individual item(s) above. Here we will give some examples of groups of columns (colonnades) in various parts and times in Ancient Egypt.

1. At Saqqara

There are forty columns in the colonnade at the Pyramid Complex of Zoser. Originally, the colonnade was roofed in. The roof over the shorter end columns formed a long, T-shaped gallery. The columns of the colonnade are popularly called *fluted*, which is technically incorrect. They are reeded or fasciculated, which varied in width between top and bottom.

These columns are peculiar in that they are attached to the main wall by connecting masonry. To suggest that the connecting walls were needed because the Egyptians lacked the technical capability to design freestanding columns is incomprehensible. It is difficult to imagine that the Egyptians, with their innumerable innovations at Saqqara, would be incapable of building a rather elementary freestanding column, if they wanted to.

This form of design at Saqqara allows for more efficient design. On an aesthetic level, it provides beautiful cubical areas.

The number game here is fascinating, as they relate to Osiris. There are 40 columns in total. Most of them have 17 stalks. Towards the end, the double freestanding columns at the western end have 19 stalks.

The number 17 represents the day Osiris died. The number 19 represents his resurrection in the western skies.

As the colonnade progresses west, the distance between the columns also narrows. With the superb Egyptian knowledge of harmony and proportion, there must be a deeper purpose to this narrowing than sheer artistry.

2. At the Karnak Temple

a. Grand Hypostyle Hall

The grand Hypostyle Hall is the structure that, along with the Great Pyramid and the Sphinx, has won universal recognition as one of the world's greatest architectural masterpieces. Here, in this Hypostyle Hall, all aspects of creation—religion, philosophy, science and art—are realized in the stones. The result, aesthetically, is overpowering.

There are seven rows of nine columns on each side of the double row of six higher columns in the center. This emphasis upon six, seven, and nine is found nowhere else in Egypt. Seven, the number of process and growth, is multiplied by nine. Nine, the Ennead, is a reiterated theme of Ancient Egypt. The Great Ennead is responsible for bringing the Universe into being, and sustaining it.

Nowhere in the world is there a more eminent or nobler architectural conception, or one carried out with such superior effectiveness, than the Hypostyle Hall at the Karnak Temple.

b. The Festival Temple of Twthomosis III

The columns here are tapered in reverse; narrower at the bottom than at the top. The style of these columns, together with their capitals, are shaped in reversed calyxes, giving this temple a special, tent-like effect.{See details of this form in Chapter 11 of this book]

3. At the Luxor Temple

a. The Colonnade of Amenhotep III consists of a double row of seven smooth-budded capital columns. Seven is the number symbolizing process. The tall, graceful columns represent clustered papyrus stalks with budded capitals.

b. The Hypostyle Hall consists of 32 densely packed columns. The paving stone of the floor at the base of the columns shows the chiseled successive phases of the moon. The moon is new, at the southernmost row of columns. The second row shows the crescent moon. The third and fourth rows show the growing size of the moon... up to a full size.

6.7 THE OBELISKS

The Egyptian obelisk is made of one piece of pink granite. Like all the pink granite of Egypt, it was quarried several hundred miles to the south, at Aswan, transported several miles to the river, loaded onto a cargo ship, floated down to Luxor (Thebes), and then set up on its pedestal with perfect accuracy.

Many of these obelisks found their way to Europe and America and into their more prominent cities.

Ritual reliefs show the Pharaoh single-handedly raising an obelisk by means of a single rope tied to its upper extremity. This is, of course, symbolic. According to the famed Egyptologist Franqois Daumas, the erection of the obelisk was a symbolic reproduction of the Tet (djed) pillar, the familiar Osirian symbol standing for the backbone (support) of the physical world and the channel through which the divine spirit might rise through matter to rejoin its source.

But did the obelisk just have a symbolic function, or did it also serve a scientific function?

Having two obelisks at the entrance to the temples and having them consistently of different height and dimensions (where symmetry would seem the natural procedure) have suggested possible scientific functions.

Upon careful measurements and analysis, it was found that although the obelisks appear perfectly square, they are not. Their edges form angles that are slightly out of square, and in a device cut as precisely as an obelisk, this cannot be accidental. Some suggested that this slight angle variation, along with the dimensions of the obelisk and the angles of the pyramidion (the pyramid-shaped top, originally plated in electrum, an alloy of gold and silver), is all calculated according to geodetic data pertaining to the exact longitude and latitude where the obelisk was originally set. This would make the obelisk much more than a simple sundial.

The shadows cast by the pair of unequal obelisks at the entrance to a temple would enable the astronomer/priests to obtain precise calendrical and astronomical data relevant to this given location. Egyptians were then able to coordinate such data with similar readings from other key sites which are also furnished with their peculiar obelisks.

6.8 STATUARY FORMS

Statuary as Dwelling Images

An image is defined as *a physical likeness or representation of a person, animal, or thing*, photographed, painted, sculptured, or otherwise made visible.

As discussed earlier in Chapter 2 of this book [*The Metaphysical Structure of the Universe*], lighter forms of energies/spirits may occupy, at will, a more condensed energy (matter) such as human, animal, plant, or any form.

The spirit/energy matrix that animated the human flesh/ matter at birth and left the body (matter) at death can likewise reside in any other matter for as long as it wants to. In order to communicate with a departed (free) spirit, a dwelling place (a condensed form of energy, possibly matter) is needed, in order for the free spirit to manifest and communicate its will and influence to the living beings on Earth. Neteru (gods, goddesses) and ancestral spirits possessed places in which to dwell, and they were believed to enter and leave their statues at will. Therefore, the Ancient and Baladi Egyptians provide dwelling places for spirits of all kinds in the form of statues and amulets.

Neither the Ancient Egyptian nor their Baladi descendants believed in the divinity of their statues. These objects are simply local residences. A spirit (energy matrix) can live anywhere, and in anything. The thing itself, the material itself, is nothing more than a medium. The user makes a clear distinction between a certain material object and the spirit, for the time inhabiting it.

For this reason, nothing is too small or too ridiculous to be considered fit for a spirit's local residence; for when the spirit is supposed to have gone out of that thing (vacates it) and definitely abandons it, the object itself is discarded and thrown away as useless.

Personal Statuary Images

The Egyptians prepared a figure or statue of the deceased person, taking great pains to give it all the characteristics of the deceased so that the 'Ka' might recognize it as an image of its body and be pleased to enter into the figure and take up its abode there. As such, these 'Ka statues' acted as the temporary host/dwelling/residence of the individual's migrating soul [Ba] which can come and visit it with the proper rituals at specific times of the year.

These personal images were placed in some safe place in the tomb—in the so-called serdab (the word signifies 'cellar'). As it was not possible to have a serdab in a grotto tomb, the statues of the deceased were placed in a niche of the furthermost chamber.

Statuary Images in Temples

Several statue types with their corresponding functions—inside the Egyptian temple as well as those placed along the processional ways or before the pylon – fulfilled several functions. Such statues acted as potential 'hosts' in which divine forces could reside, with the proper rituals.

Such statues acted also as intermediaries between the people and

the neteru (gods, goddesses) in return for pronouncing the name
and reciting the offering formula. The most potent of all the statues in the temple was the effigy at the focal point of the temple,
representing the 'Ka' of the neter [divine force]. The effigy acted
as the 'body' (being a condensed form of energy) for which the
'Ba' comes back to; the 'Ka' being the vital force of the spiritual
manifestation of the neter [divine force], which is recognized by
its 'Ba'.

Statues and effigies in temples served as dwelling places for the
neteru/cosmic energies. These statues were carefully designed to
match each neter's exact replica.

A passage from the stele of King Neferhotep (5,000 years ago) at
Abydos describes his plan to seek original information from the
archives about the exact traditional form of the statue of Osiris:

> *I will fashion [him, his limbs-his face, his fingers] according to
> that which my person has seen in the rolls of his [forms].*

Conceptual Cubical Statues

Conceptual-type statues do not represent a specific person, but a
certain conception and/or divine powers.

The Egyptian was highly conscious of the box-like structure
which is the model of the Earth or the material world. Cube statues are found in the earliest discovered Ancient Egyptian monuments where the form of statuary called the *cube statue* was
common. The subject was integrated into the cubic form of the
stone. In some of these cube statues, there is a powerful sense of
the subject emerging from the prison of the cube. The statue, as
such, signifies that the spiritual principle is emerging from the
material world.

The 'king'—as the divine man [in Christianity: Son of God] – is often shown sitting on a cubic throne or seat, signifying the spiritual principle of domination and triumph over the material.

Other traditions, such as the Platonic and Pythagorean, adopted the same concept of the Egyptian cubic representation of the material world.

Conceptual Statues of Human and/or Animal Forms

So many phrases are being used throughout the world which consistently state that the human being is made in the image of God (a miniature universe) and that to understand the universe is to understand oneself, and vice versa – yet, no culture has ever practiced the above principle like the Ancient Egyptians. Central to their complete understanding of the universe was the knowledge that man was made in the image of God, and as such, man represented the image of all creation.

Animal forms embody certain divine functions and principles, as explained earlier in the discussion about animal symbolism. There were three main representations in such conceptual statuary images. The first and second are animal-headed humans or a pure animal form. The third form is the opposite of an animal-headed human, being that of a human-headed animal/bird—the divine aspect of the terrestrial.

Material Types

The choice of stone type was neither necessitated by economics nor by practical structural consideration. It is believed that each stone type represents specific aspects of the cosmic process. Here are the cosmic representations of some stones:

Alabaster = Air
Sandstone = Earth
Limestone = Water
Granite = Fire

A very common proof of such a choice is that the lioness netert (goddess) Sekhmet statues are made of granite, representing fire.

[See Appendix F—Sculpture—for more elaboration on a few Egyptian sculptures.]

6.9 ROOF FORMS

To roof the building, the Ancient Egyptians used all types of ceilings that continue to be used nowadays. The type of roof was dictated by metaphysical reasons and not construction practicality.

For various functions, they have used:

1. A Flat roof—supported on a system of beams that are supported on columns or bearing walls

At Zoser complex, the ceiling of the entrance passage simulates a roof of split logs. Similar imitations of organic originals are present in many Egyptian buildings.

2. Gabled roofing

The word gable is of Egyptian origin, which is *Gabal*, meaning the top/peak of a mountain – i.e. the shape is triangular, as shown above, earlier.

Gabled roofing is found in many monuments of the Old Kingdom, about 4,500 years ago.

3. Corbelled Roofing—a 'false' arch/vault

This form of stone roofing was like a stepped arch,as found inside the Great Pyramid in two locations:

  – as the roof of the so-called *Queen's Room*

  – as the roof of the Grand Gallery.

This roofing form was also utilized in the earlier Snefru pyramids.

Also, check similar applications in earlier photos in various parts of this book.

4. Arches and Vaulted Ceilings

The Ancient Egyptians utilized arches and vaulted roofs in their buildings since their earliest history. It is a good idea to take a minute to review the actual definition of an arch and a vault.

According to the definition in the dictionary, **an arch is** *a typically curved structural member spanning an opening and serving as a support (as for the wall or other weight above the opening): a) something resembling an arch in form of function: esp: either of two vaulted portions of the bony structure of the foot that impart elasticity to it; b) a curvature having the form of an arch.*

The vault is: *a) an arched structure of masonry usually forming a ceiling or roof; b) something (as the sky) resembling a vault; c) an arched or dome-shaped anatomical structure; d) a space covered by an arched structure: esp: an underground passage or room.*

Arches and vaults are found in all eras in Egyptian temples and other large buildings, being above or below ground.

The vaulted ceiling is a reflection of the netert (goddess) Nut—*the firmament* – and therefore, burial chambers are vaulted (or gabled, in Old Kingdom).

The earliest stone arch is found in Saqqara. A papyrus that was found in Zoser's Pyramid Complex (3rd Dynasty) at Saqqara shows the definition of the curve of a roof by a system of coordinates. The vertical lines are shown placed at equal distances from one another, while the numbers indicate their length from an unmarked horizontal level and define the coordinates of a number of points on the curve. This is proof that the Egyptians had a very exact idea of graphic representation at least 5,000 years ago.

In addition to the arch found in Saqqara, many others are also found in and near the pyramids of Giza, 4,500 years ago.

Crude brick arches were commonly used in roofing tombs since its earliest times, at least as far back as 1600 BCE, in Luxor (Thebes). Other arches are found from the times of Tuthomosis III and of Ramses V.

An arch, being of stone, is no stronger proof of its existence than are those of brick at Luxor (Thebes). **The principle of the arch is the same, regardless of the material used**. Basically, the brick arch (like the stone) radiates to a common center. It is not necessary that an arch should be of any particular material; nor does the arch have to have a keystone to be qualified as an "arch". Arches, both round and pointed, are found at all eras, without a keystone. The same was the case in Ancient Egypt.

All shapes, types, and materials (brick, stone, etc.) of arches can be found in Ancient Egypt centuries and even millennia before Greek and Roman times.

A **vaulted roof** is found in the Pyramid of Menkaura in Giza, which is about 4,500 years old. Another vaulted roof is found in the Pharaoh's monument, following Menkaura, in the structure called *Mastabat-Faroon* in Saqqara.

We also find **several perfectly-fitted vaulted roofs** further south, in the very remote temple in Abydos.

The roof here is formed of single blocks of stone reaching from one architrave to the other which, instead of being placed in the usual manner, stand upon their edges in order to allow room for hollowing out an arch in their thickness.

A perfectly-constructed series of arches or vaulted ceilings at the Ramesseum temple on Luxor's west bank is 3,500 years old.

The Egyptians used a **wide variety of curved roofs.**

The arch can be circular or with other variations of curvature. In addition to above examples, here is another one:

The above were a general characterization of various shapes and forms. The Egyptian utilized these forms in a wide range, from simple applications to a more stylized application, and in a varying degree of stylization from a simple paintings to body formations. All such stylizations were consistent with the main objective/function and were intended to enhance and amplify each's function.

6.10 STYLISTIC ARCHITECTURAL DETAILS

Several stylistic architectural features were also used in Ancient Egypt, such as:

Architrave – The architrave was derived in Egypt from the stone beam, reaching from pillar to pillar in tombs and temples.

Since the 1st dynasty, the smallest private tomb-mastaba has a typical architrave above the entrance doorway.

The stone architrave was used to increase the size of, and add a portico to, their temples.

Square dentils over an architrave were also utilized since Egypt's earliest history and can be seen in the facade of a tomb at Beni Hassan and pm the ceiling of one of the rock tombs at the Pyramids, imitating the palm beams.

Here it is shown in beautiful detail at the Karnak Temples Complex in Luxor:

<u>Cornice</u> – It was utilized constantly as a significant detail in the design of the so-called False doors which is to be found in every tomb and temple in Ancient Egypt. Notice other features, as well.

Below is a fully painted example from a Saqqara tomb from about 45 centuries ago.

For their devices, the Egyptians frequently selected objects such as the lotus and other flowers, and these, as well as various animals or their heads, were adapted to form a cornice, particularly in their houses and tombs, or to decorate fancy articles of furniture and dress.

<u>**Torus**</u> – The torus has been used in Egypt since its recovered remotest history more than 5,000 years ago, and is shown here as a significant detail of the so-called False Door at every Egyptian tomb and temple.

6.11 STYLISTIC ORNAMENTATION AND DECORATION

Many people miss the artistic talents of the Ancient Egyptians by focusing only on the figurative depictions in Egyptian buildings.

Some artistic variations are noticed by some, but even, then we are told that the Egyptians had *no imagination* and therefore could only imitate nature, such as these palm tree column caps that look like the abundant palm trees in Egypt.

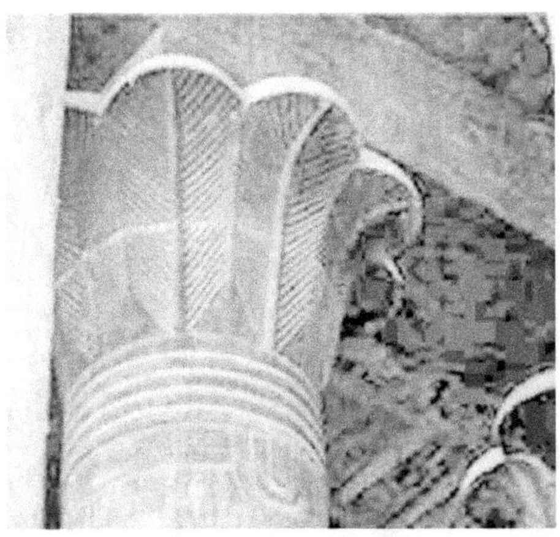

The design patterns in Egypt can generally be categorized as floral, geometric, figurative, or a combination of two or all three.

The <u>**figurative patterns**</u> naturally dominate temples and tombs; but floral and geometric patterns are abundant.

The Western mind set is obsessed with giving names to every variation of these patterns and to attaching a Greek/Roman adjective to each, despite its pre-existence in Egypt.

The **floral** type is depicted in a range of plant maturity, from the closed bud to the open blossom.

Geometric design patterns are all over, from the starry ceilings to all kinds of patterns in tombs and temples everywhere in Egypt— long before they found their way to Europe.Such patterns consisted of one,or a combination of 2 or all three forms of decorations—floral, geometric, and figurative.

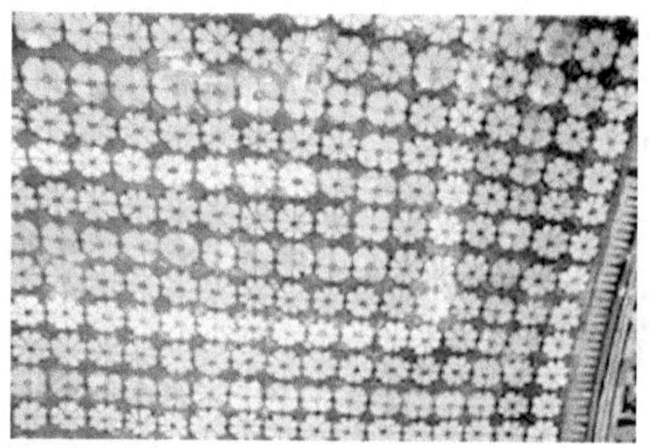

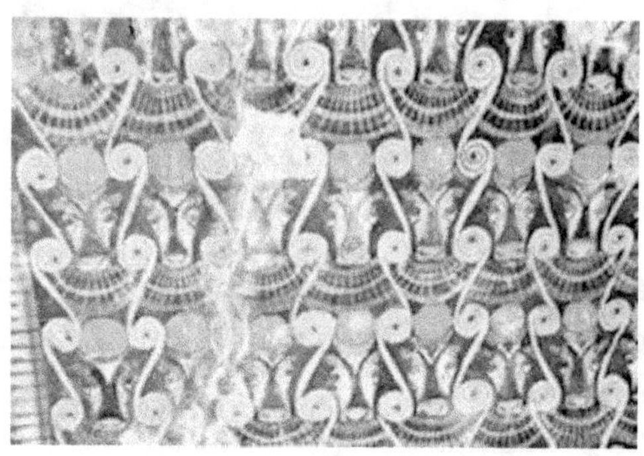

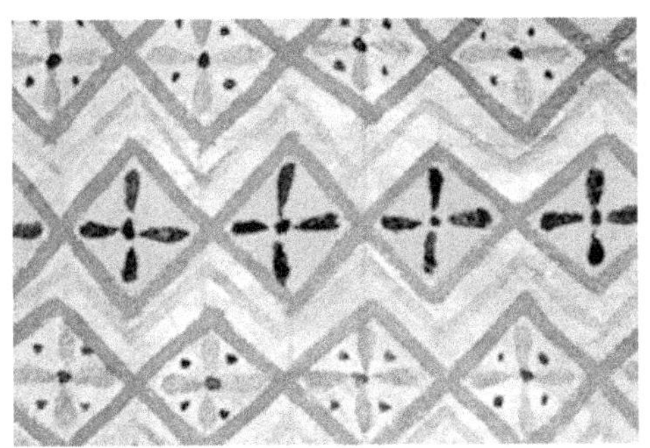

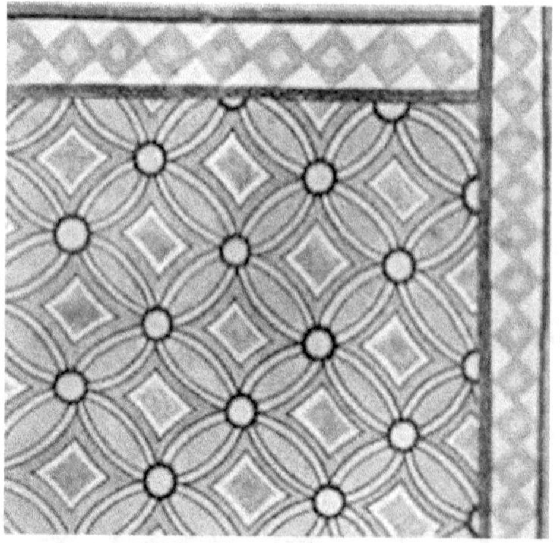

Egyptians did not always confine themselves to the mere imitation of natural objects for ornament.

Their ceilings and cornices offer numerous graceful fancy devices; among which are the guilloche (misnamed as the Tuscan border), the chevron, and the scroll pattern.

These items can be seen in a tomb dating back to the 6th Dynasty; they were therefore known in Egypt many ages before they were later adopted by the Greeks and Romans.

Guilloche – The most complicated form of the guilloche covered a whole Egyptian ceiling more than a thousand years before it was represented on those comparatively late objects, found at Nineveh.[shown above]

<u>**A Chevron**</u> is a type of ornament also commonly found in Ancient Egypt.[shown above]

<u>**The Scroll**</u> is also found in Ancient Egypt.[shown above]

<u>Colors</u>

Color was an essential part of Egyptian architecture.

No one who understands the harmony of colors will fail to admit that the Ancient Egyptians perfectly understood their distribution and proper combinations.

But the choice of colors—just like everything else—reflects the Egyptians' deep metaphysical understanding of the significance and energy of each color, and various colors are derived from a combination of basic colors.

The ceilings of Egyptian temples were painted blue and studded with stars to represent the firmament (as in early European churches); and on the part over the central passage (through which the king and the religious processions passed) were vultures and other emblems; the winged globe always having its place over the doorways. The whole building, as well as its sphinxes and other accessories, was richly painted.

>>> Several color photographs in support of the text of this subchapter are to be found in the digital edition of this book as published in PDF and E-book formats.

Chapter 7 : The Primary Geometrical Shapes/Forms

7.1 SACRED GEOMETRY OF DIVINE ARCHITECTURE

Geometry to the Ancient Egyptians was much more than a study of points, lines, surfaces, and solids and their properties and measurement. The harmony inherent in geometry was recognized in Ancient Egypt as the most cogent expression of a divine plan that underlies the world—a metaphysical plan that determines the physical.

To the Ancient Egyptians, geometry was the means by which humanity could understand the mysteries of the divine order. Geometry exists everywhere in nature: its order underlies the structure of all things, from molecules to galaxies. The nature of the geometric form allows its functioning. A design using the principles of sacred geometry must achieve the same goal: using form to serve/represent a function.

Herodotus, the father of history and a native Greek, stated, in 500 BCE:

> *Now, let me talk more of Egypt for it has a lot of admirable things and what one sees there is superior to any other country.*

The Ancient Egyptian's works, large or small, are admired by all because they are proportionally harmonious and, as such, appeal to our inner as well as our outer feelings. This harmonic design concept is popularly known as sacred geometry, where all figures can be drawn or created using a straight line (not even necessarily a ruler) and compass – i.e. without measurement (dependent on proportion only).

7.2 THE EGYPTIAN SACRED CORD [TOOL]

Since sacred geometry is based on harmonic proportion, the unit distance (length) can theoretically be any unit. The only needed tool is a cord consisting of 12 equally spaced distances. The unit distance can be small or large, so as to fit the required design of artwork on a canvas, statues, or the layout of buildings.

Temples and other buildings in Ancient Egypt were laid out in a religious ceremony. This laying out was performed by very knowledgeable people who are known to the Greeks as *harpedonaptae*.

The harpedonaptae are the people who strictly adhered to the principles of sacred geometry (using only a straight line and a compass). Their cord was (and still is, in parts of present-day Egypt) a very special cord that consists of a 13-knot rope with 12 equally-spaced distances of one Egyptian cubit (1.72′ or 0.5236 m).

Any equally-spaced 13-knot cord is the basic tool used to establish various geometric shapes.

7.3 GENERAL LAYOUT OF GEOMETRIC SHAPES

Triangles are the building blocks of any design.

The simplest formation is the equilateral triangle, which can be set out with the Egyptian rope knotted at twelve equal intervals and wound around three pegs so that it formed three sides, each measuring four units.

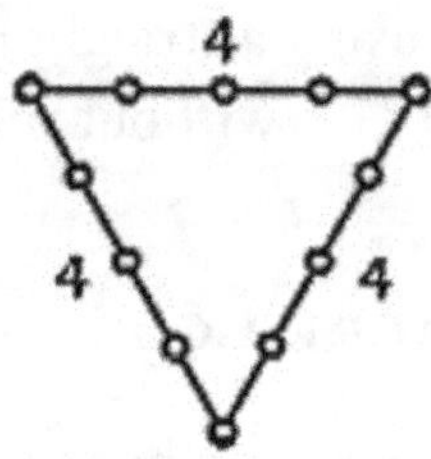

The line joining from any corner to the middle of the opposite side is its perpendicular.

However, the origin of the historic building layout was the setting out of the 3:4:5 triangle with the Egyptian rope, wound around three pegs so that it formed three sides measuring three, four, and five units, which provides a 90° angle between its 3 and 4 sides.

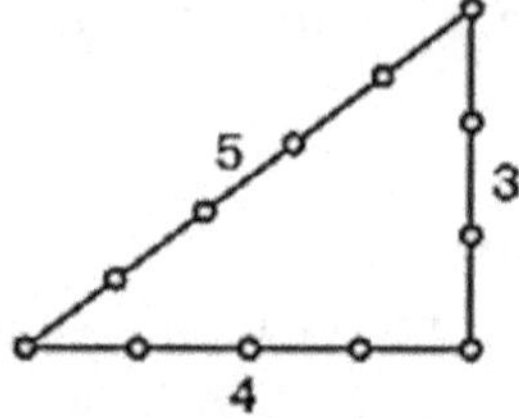

It was a relatively simple task to lay out rectangles and other more complex geometrical figures after establishing the 3:4:5 right-angle triangle.

A square EBCF, for example, can be established as shown herein:

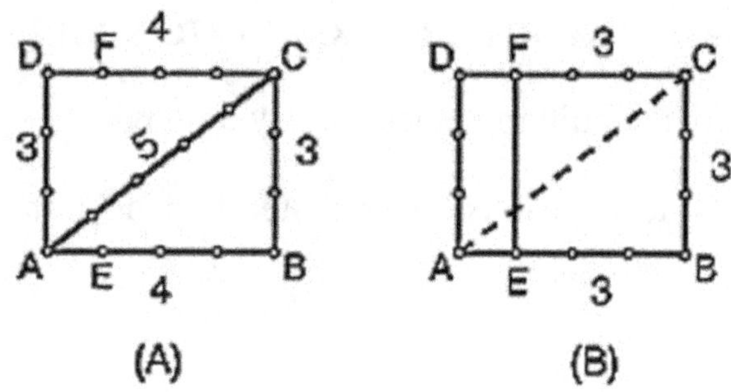

(A) Construct two 3:4:5 triangles with a common diagonal AC.

(B) Connect FE where FC = EB = 3 units.

The Egyptian cord can be used as a compass to draw circular curves, as shown in the diagram below.

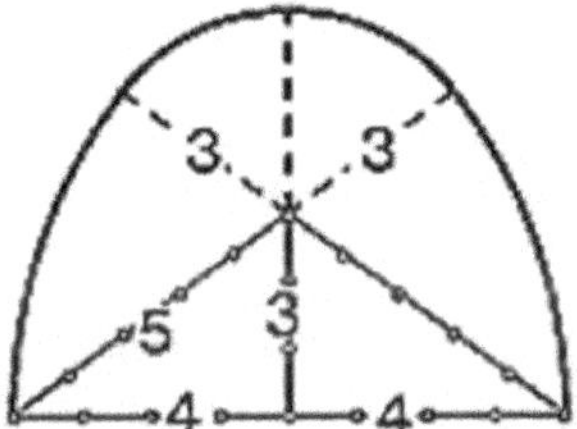

Other shapes, such as the 8:5 Neb (Golden) triangle or rectangle, as shown below, can also be established with the Egyptian cord.

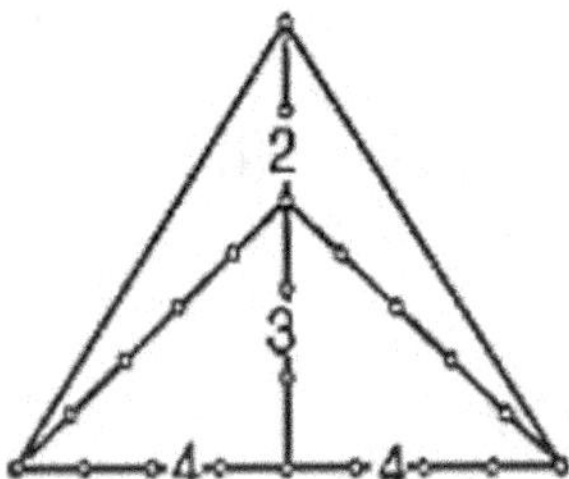

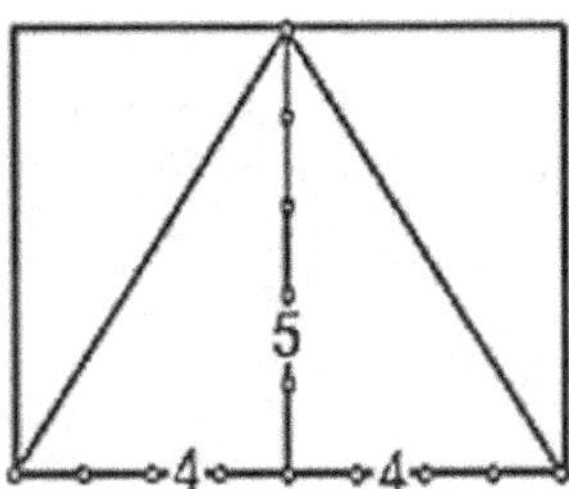

[To see the formation of a wide variety of geometrical shapes, read *Sacred Geometry and Numerology* by this same author.]

The hieroglyphic symbol for the neter (god) Re, the cosmic creative force, is the circle. When the cord is looped as a full circle, the archetype of creation, we find that the radius of this sacred circle equals 1.91 cubits. In converting this measurement of 1.91 cubits of the radius into the metric system, we get 1 meter exactly (1.91 x 0.5236). 1 meter = 1/100,000th – part of the quarter of the Earth's meridian. In other words, this particular 13-knotted Egyptian rope and the Egyptian unit of measurement known as a cubit are based on the measurement of the Earth's circumference.

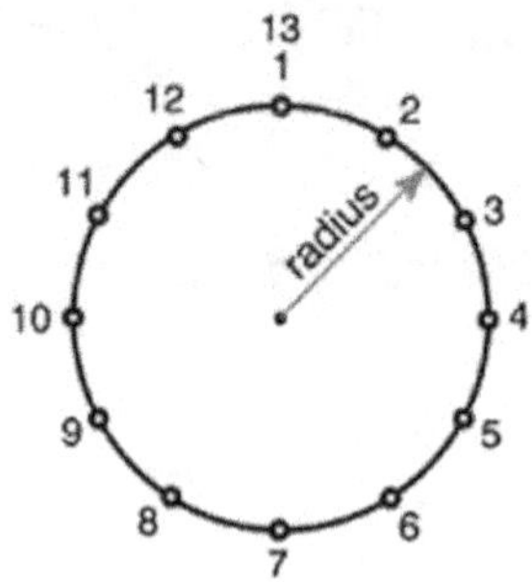

Throughout this book, you will find this cord to be the only tool needed to establish all sacred geometric shapes, from a straight line to a curve to other shapes.

7.4 THE SACRED CIRCLE OF RE

The cosmic creative force Re is written as a circle with a dot or point in the center. It is a circle moving in a circle, one and solitary. The circle symbolically represents the Absolute, or undifferentiated, Unity.

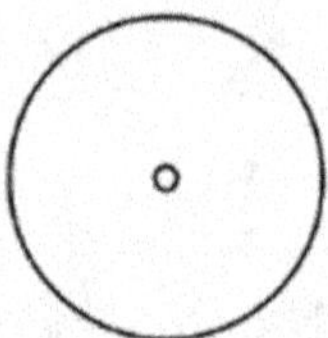

The Circle Index is the functional representation of the circle. It is the ratio between the circumference of the circle to its diameter. It is popularized by Western academia by the Greek letter pi and given a value of 3.1415927.

The Circle Index and the Neb (Golden) Proportion were seen by the Ancient Egyptians not in numerical terms, but as emblematic of the creative or generative function. One cannot just reduce a process/function to a meaningless, unmeasurable "value" and then call it an "irrational number".

The Ancient Egyptians were not interested in abstract "number gymnastics".

That the Ancient Egyptians knew how to inscribe a polygon within a circle is proven beyond doubt by their invention of capitals and column shafts that are polygonal in cross-section.

The Egyptians built their capitals with nine elements (and occasionally with seven), in addition to 6, 8, 11, and 13-sided polygons, because they knew the properties of the circle and its relationship to perpendicular coordinates and other geometric figures. Their executed work is sufficient evidence of such knowledge.

The Egyptians manifested their knowledge of the circle properties and other curves as early as their surviving records. A 3rd Dynasty (~2630 BCE) record shows the definition of the curve of a roof in Saqqara by a system of coordinates.

This shows that their knowledge of the circle enabled them to calculate the coordinates along this vertical curve. Accordingly, the construction workers followed precise dimensions in their executed circular curves.

Such an application was evident in Egypt at least 2,000 years before Archimedes walked this earth.

7.5 SQUARING THE CIRCLE—THE MANIFESTATION OF CREATION

"Squaring the circle" for the Ancient Egyptians represented the realization of creation—the transformation process of the concept of creation into its actual manifestation.

Such transformation is reflected and evident in all Ancient Egyptian "mathematical" papyri. In all these papyri, the area of a circle was obtained by **squaring the circle**. The diameter was always represented as 9 cubits. The Ancient Egyptian papyri equates the 9-cubit diameter circle to a square with the sides of 8 cubits.

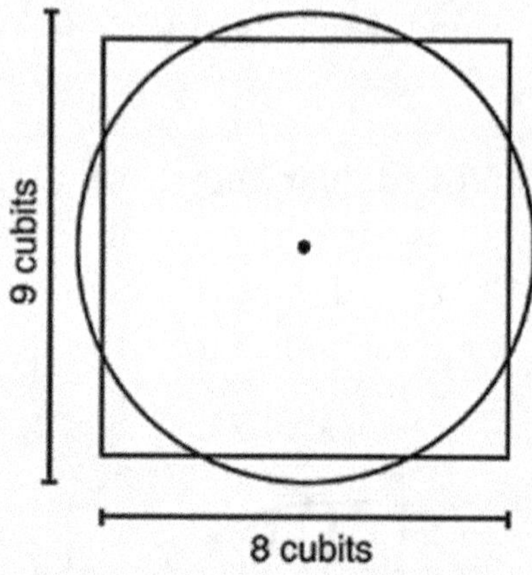

The number 9, as the diameter, represents the Ennead, the group of 9 neteru (gods, goddesses) who produced the ingredients of creation. The 9 are all aspects of Re, the primeval cosmic creative force whose symbol is/was the circle.

8 corresponds to the physical world as we experience it. 8 is the number of Thoth, and at Khmunu (Hermopolis), Thoth is known as the **Master of the City of Eight.**

Musically, the ratio 8:9 is the Perfect Tone. The 8:9 ratio is present in Ancient Egyptian works, such as the proportion of the inner chamber of the top sanctuary at Luxor Temple.

The underlying metaphysical patterns of the manifested universe are represented in the relationship of **squaring the circle** (Re and Thoth—conceived and manifested).

Thoth transformed the creation concept (symbolized in a circle) into a physical and metaphysical reality. Such transformation is reflected in the Ancient Egyptian process of "squaring the circle".

The area of a circle with 9 cubits as its diameter = 63.61725.

The area of the squared circle with 8 cubits as its side = 64.

The difference = 64 − 63.61725 = 0.38.

Such a difference = 0.6%, which reflects the Ancient Egyptian consideration of a slight deviation from perfection in the manifested world.

A good example of this slight imperfection is the orbit of the Earth around the sun, which follows an elliptical shape and not a perfect circle.

Musically, the ratio 8:9 is the Perfect Tone.

The ratio 8:9 = 2 to its 3rd power and 3 to its 2nd power. This is the perfect relationship between the reciprocals of 2 and 3 to their reciprocal powers of 3 and 2. The numbers 2 and 3 are the two primary cosmic numbers, as will be discussed in Chapter 9 of this book.

The walls of the Egyptian temple were covered with animated images—including hieroglyphs—to facilitate the communication between the above and the below.

The Ancient Egyptian framework was usually a square, representing the manifested world (squaring of the circle). Additionally, the square grid itself had symbolic meaning for the manifested world, which also made it easy to construct the root rectangles of 2, 3, and 5, on/by the square(s) background. The corners of squares and root rectangles were defined by notches along the perimeter or carefully defined by incised lines.

7.6 TRIANGLES

The following is an overview of the geometric configuration of three Egyptian triangles.

The Thoth (Ibis) Triangle

Plutarch, in his *Moralia Vol. V* about Ancient Egypt, wrote:

> *By the spreading of Ibis' feet, in their relation to each other and to her bill, she makes an equilateral triangle.*

Ibis is the sacred bird of Thoth, whose words created the world.

An equilateral triangle could be set out with the Egyptian rope knotted at twelve equal intervals and wound about three pegs so that it formed three sides, each measuring four units.

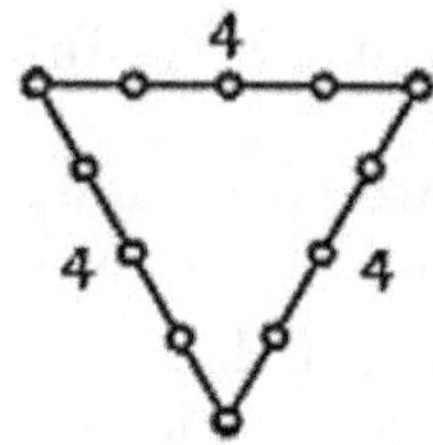

The line joining from any corner to the middle of the opposite side is its perpendicular. With the Egyptian cord, all perpendiculars can be established without any measurements whatsoever.

The Osiris (Union) Triangle

The 3:4:5 triangle, where the height is to the base as 3 is to 4, was called the "Osiris" Triangle by Plutarch. This triangle was set out with the Egyptian rope, wound about three pegs so that it formed three sides measuring three, four, and five units, which provides a 90° angle between its 3 and 4 sides.

It is a historical lie to call it the Pythagorean Triangle. It was used in Ancient Egypt for thousands of years before Pythagoras walked this earth. It is very clear, from Plutarch's testimony below, that the ancient Egyptians knew that 3:4:5 is a right-angle triangle, since 3 is called 'upright' and 4 is 'the base', forming a 90° angle. Plutarch wrote about the 3:4:5 right-angle triangle of ancient Egypt in *Moralia, Vol. V*:

> *The Egyptians hold in high honor the most beautiful of the triangles, since they liken the nature of the Universe most closely to it, as Plato in the Republic seems to have made use of it in formulating his figure of marriage. This triangle has its upright of three units, its base of four, and its hypotenuse of five, whose power is equal to that of the other two sides. The upright, therefore, may be likened to the male, the base to the female, and the hypotenuse to the child of both, and so Osiris may be regarded as the origin, Isis as the recipient, and Horus as perfected result. Three is the first perfect odd number: four is a square whose side is the even number two; but five is in some ways like to its father, and in some ways like to its mother, being made up of three and two. And panta (all) is a derivative of pente (five), and they speak of counting as "numbering by fives". Five makes a square of itself.*

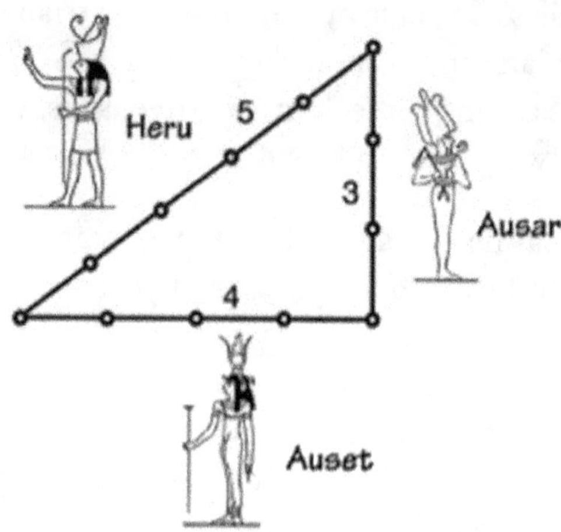

The Neb (Golden) Triangle

The Neb (Golden) triangle, which is commonly known as 5:8 isosceles triangle, is by far the most widely used in constructional and harmonic diagram in Egyptian architecture and art, and it was no whim for Viollet-le-Duc to call it **the Egyptian Triangle**.

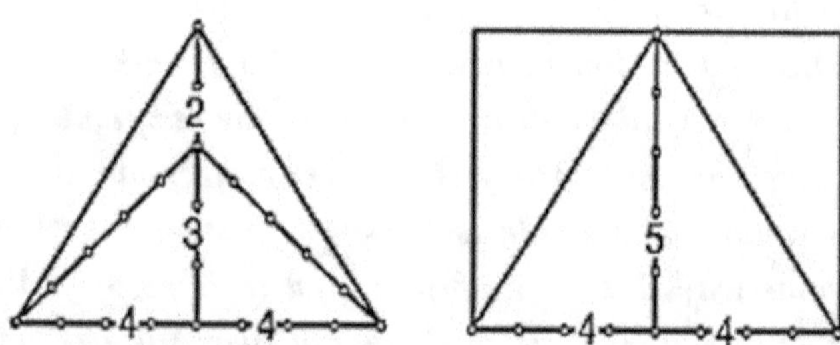

Numerous Egyptian amulets, representing the mason's level, have been discovered and are now scattered throughout the museums of the world (Turin, Louvre, etc.). The Neb (Golden) triangle represents the greatest percentage of these shapes which included the 3:4:5 right-angle triangle and equilateral triangle.

7.7 THE COMBINED SQUARE-TRIANGLES 3-D PYRAMIDS

The pyramid shape consists of a square base and triangle volume.

For detailed information about the configurations and the associated sacred geometric designs of the Egyptian masonry pyramids, read *Egyptian Pyramids Revisited* by Moustafa Gadalla.

Chapter 8 : The Generative Square Root Rectangles

8.1 THE ROOT RECTANGLES—FROM CIRCLE TO SQUARE TO RECTANGLES

The role of a root in a plant is the same exact role/function as that of the root in geometry. The root of a plant assimilates, generates, and transforms energies to the rest of the plant.

Likewise, the geometric root is an archetypal expression of the assimilative, generating, transformative function and process, whereas fixed whole numbers are the structures that emerge to build upon these principles of process.

As stated earlier, the concept of creation was manifested in the act of squaring the sacred circle of Re. The square is the basic geometric shape from which all root rectangles can be generated.

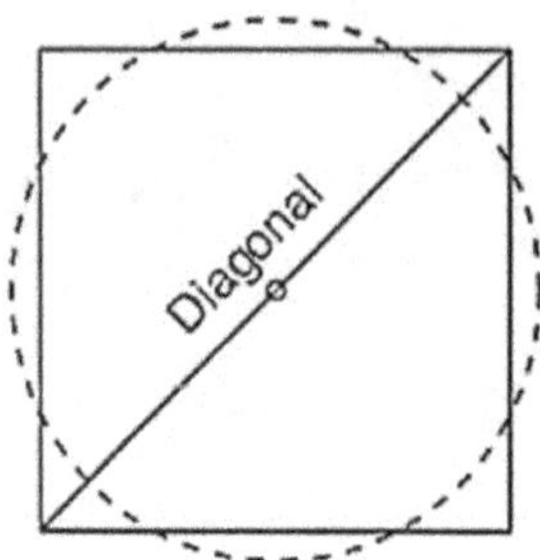

The diagonals serve as the generators of root rectangles. When we start with a square whose side is one, the diagonal is $\sqrt{2}$. From the square root of two, other root rectangles are produced directly by simply drawing with compasses, i.e. applying sacred geometry (producing without measurement) by using squares and rectangles and their diagonals.

The Ancient Egyptians were able to obtain root rectangles without measurements through various ways, such as:

- Start with a square whose side is unity.

- The √2 rectangle is produced from the square by setting the compass at the length of the diagonal and producing the base line to meet it. This makes the length of the long side equal to the square root of 2, taking the short side as unity.

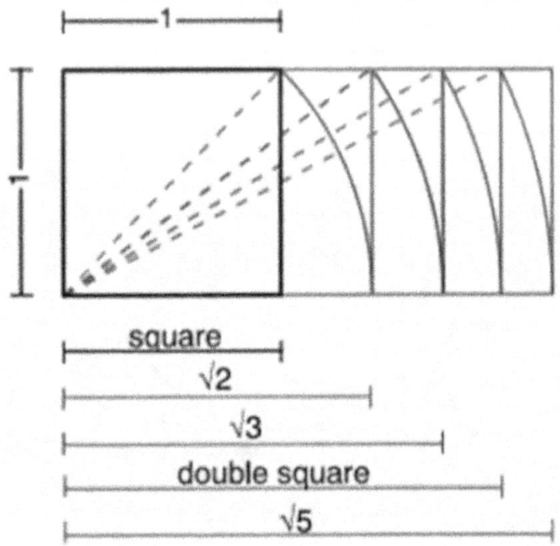

- The √3 rectangle is produced from the diagonal of the √2 rectangle.

- The √4 rectangle (double square) is produced from the diagonal of the √3 rectangle.

- The √5 rectangle is produced from the double square rectangle.

Design that is based on root rectangles is called generative dynamic design, which only the Egyptians practiced. Egyptian sacred objects and buildings have geometries based upon the division of space attained by the root rectangles and their derivatives, such as the Neb (Golden) Proportion, as will be shown throughout this book.

8.2 THE COSMIC SOLIDS

From the roots of Two, Three, and Five, all harmonic proportions and relationships can be derived. The interplay of these proportions and relations commands the forms of all matter—organic and inorganic—and all processes and sequences of growth.

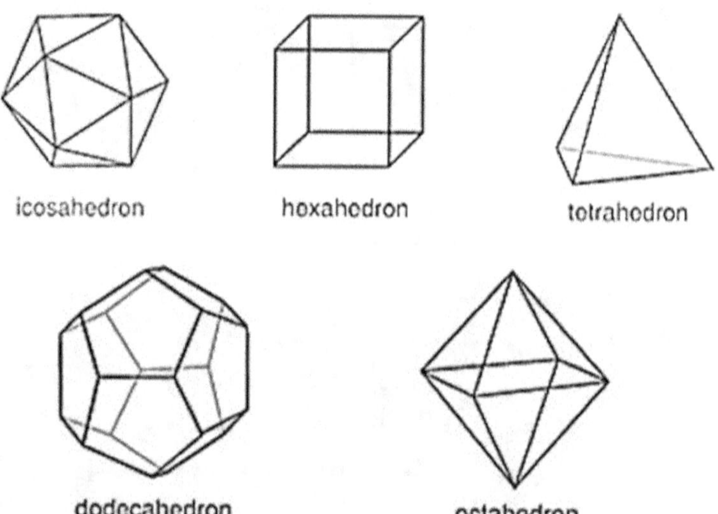

The three sacred roots are all that are necessary for the formation of the five cosmic solids [shown above] which are the basis for all volumetric forms (where all edges and all interior angles are equal). The manifestation of these five volumes are generated from the Egyptian Ennead.

8.3 THE GENERATIVE 1:2 RECTANGLE—THE DOUBLE SQUARES

As stated earlier, the circle is the archetype of creation in Ancient Egypt. Dividing the circle by its diameter produces the 1:2 ratio, which is the musical octave. The manifested world through this division is symbolized by the inscribed two equal squares, representing the balance between our physical and metaphysical worlds [see diagram below].

The 1:2 geometric outline of the twin squares represents the diapason; the octave. The octave represents renewal or self-replication.

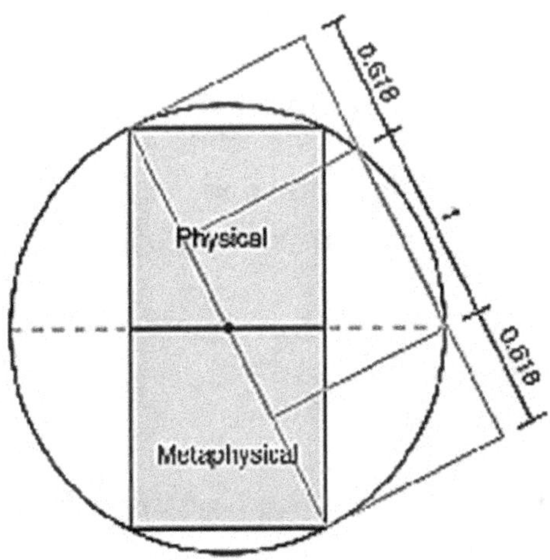

In Egyptian architectural design, the 1:2 double square rectangle assumed great importance in the elements or the general outline of the plan. Such outlines represented the octave and served as the renewal place for the physical and metaphysical well-being of the pharaoh.

• The earliest surviving of such 1:2 rectangular complexes is the Zoser Complex (2630–2611 BCE) at Saqqara. This vast sanctuary is in the form of a double square (1,000 x 500 cubits) whose walls are oriented exactly along the cardinal directions. It contains the Step Pyramid, several buildings, colonnades, and temples.

It was a very active site for all successive Pharaohs. The main function of the Zoser sanctuary was to serve as the Heb-Sed site.

Heb-Sed was the most important festival, from the point of view of the Kingship. Being a divine medium, the Egyptian King was not supposed (or even able) to reign unless he was in good health. The Heb-Sed festival was a rejuvenation of the King's vital force.

This vast sanctuary set the pattern for later holy places in Egypt and elsewhere, such as:

- The Festival Hall (Akh-Menu) of Tuthomosis III at the Karnak Temple was also used for the Heb-Sed Festival. It also consists of double-square outlines.

- On the vertical plane, the doorways of the Ancient Egyptian temples were also proportioned 1:2.

The Neb (Golden) Proportion is obtained from the diagonal of by a rectangle with sides of 1:2—the root-five diagonal. [More details later in this book.]

8.4 GENERATING ROOT RECTANGLES FROM THE DOUBLE SQUARE

From a double square, all three sacred square roots can also be obtained, as shown herein.

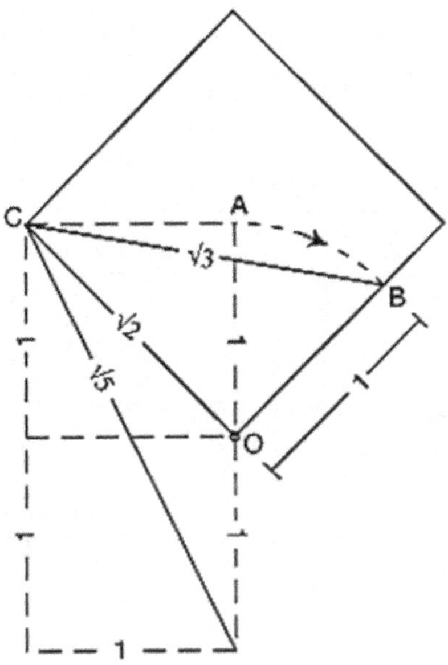

√2 is the diagonal of a square.

√3 is obtained from the √2 square by setting on point O and drawing an arc with a radius = the side of the original square (OA), at point A, to meet the side of the √2 square at B. In the right angle triangle COB, the hypotenuse CB = the square root of $[(\sqrt{2})^2 + (1)^2] = [\sqrt{(2 + 1)}] = \sqrt{3}$.

√5 is the diagonal of a double square.

• • •

• A double square [1:2 rectangle] could be obtained from two intersecting circles as each's circumference passes through the center of the other circle.

• The three sacred square roots are shown herein:

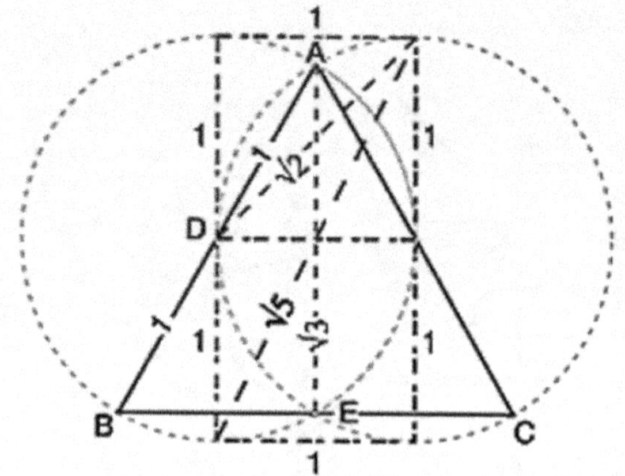

In the equilateral triangle ABC, the perpendicular line AE = √3, since the base = 1 and the hypotenuse = 2. As such, a hexagon could be drawn by utilizing AD and DE as two sides of the hexagon that can be drawn on the right circle on the right side. Two of the remaining four sides can be drawn from A and E with an arc = AD = ED, to points C and F.

From point F as a center, draw an arc with the same length of the hexagon side, to intersect the circle at point G—the sixth point on the hexagon.

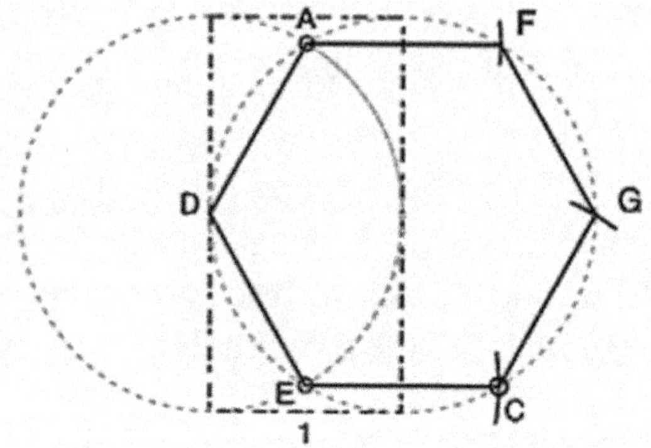

8.5 THE ROOT FIVE RECTANGLE AND THE GOLDEN PROPORTION

The √5 rectangle is obtained from the double square. The diagonal of the 1:2 rectangle is √5.

To find the relationship between the root five rectangle and the Golden Proportion (N), begin from a basic square (the manifested universe), such as DAIJ.

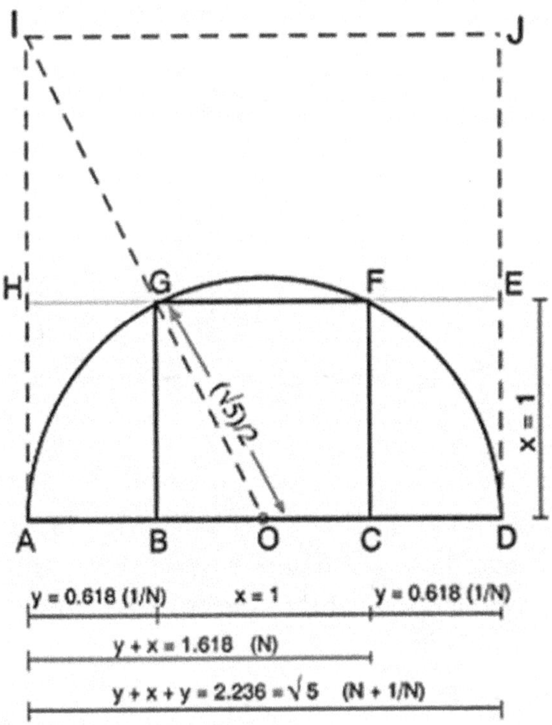

- Find the midpoint (O) between edges A and D.

- Draw a semi-circle from center O with a radius OA.

- From the intersecting point G, establish the square GBCF.

- Extend GF to H and E. The rectangle ADEH is a root five rectangle that contains two combinations:

1. Two reciprocal Neb (Golden) rectangles: ACFH (1 x 1.618) and CDEF (1 x 0.618).

2. A square (BCFG) plus two lateral Neb (Golden) rectangles. ABGH and CDEF—each is proportioned 1:0.618 (which is equal to 1.618—the Golden Proportion.

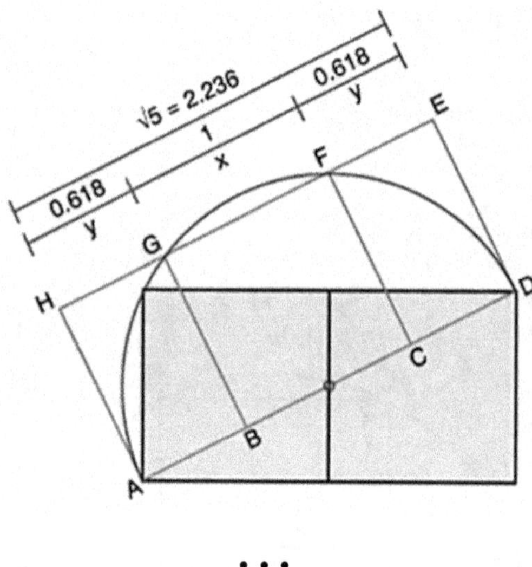

• • •

The inscribed square in the upper half of the circle represents the physical manifestation of the world. The resultant proportions were essential parts of the Ancient Egyptian design, as will be shown throughout this text.

• • •

Regarding the relationship between the square root of 5 and the five-sided pentagon, see *Sacred Geometry and Numerology* by Moustafa Gadalla.

8.6 PROPORTIONING A LINE ACCORDING TO THE GOLDEN PROPORTION

To proportion a line (say AB) according to the Neb (Golden) Proportion, establish BC = 1/2 of AB and perpendicular to it.

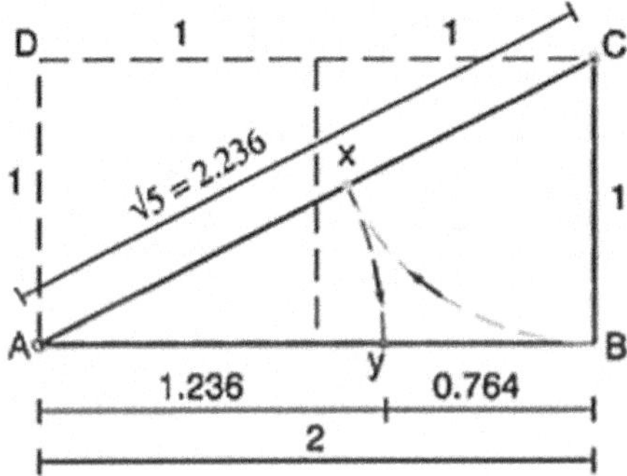

- Draw diagonal AC, which is equal to the square root of the sum of the square of the distance BC and AB:

$$\sqrt{[(BC)^2 + (AB)^2]} = \sqrt{(1+4)} = \sqrt{5}$$

- Set on corner C with an arc = CB, find the point x

    The line Cx = 1
    Therefore Ax = (2.236 − 1) = 1.236

- Set on A as a center, with a radius Ax, draw an arc to y.

    Ay = Ax = 1.236
    yB = (AB − Ay) = (2 − 1.236) = 0.764

The ratio 1.236 / 0.764 = 1.618 = The Neb (Golden) Section/Proportion (N).

This proportioning explains the uniquely reciprocal relationship between two unequal parts of a whole in which the small part stands in the same proportion to the large part as the large part stands to the whole. Such is the formula for the Neb (Golden) Section/Proportion.

The two parts of the Golden Section are often referred to as a minor and a major.

8.7 NEB: THE GOLDEN SEGMENT

Neb is an Ancient Egyptian term meaning gold (traditionally, the finished perfected end product, the goal of the alchemist), Lord, master.

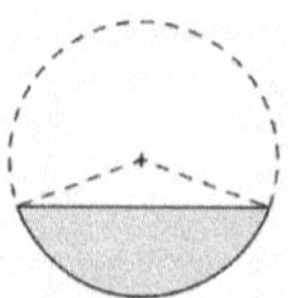

The hieroglyph denoting Neb is a segment of a circle whose central angle is 140°. The ratio of this angle to the whole circle (length of arc to whole circumference) = 0.3889, which constitutes the second power of 0.625. The second power spiritually constitutes reaching to a higher level. Neb means exactly that.

8.8 THE [WHIRLING SQUARES] SPIRALS

The spiral in nature is the result of continued proportional growth. This type of spiral is known mathematically as the constant angle or logarithmic spiral. Logarithmic expansion is the basis for the geometry of spirals. The fetus of man and animals, which are the manifestation of the generation laws, are shaped like the logarithmic spiral. Manifestations of spirals are evident in vegetable and shell growth, spider webs, the horn of the dall sheep, the trajectory of many subatomic particles, the nuclear force of atoms, the double helix of DNA, and most of all, in many of the galaxies. Patterns in the mental realm, as well, are also generated in spiraling motions.

The logarithmic spiral is the product of the combined effect of addition and multiplication, which is a progressive addition just like the Summation (Fibonacci) Series (2, 3, 5, 8, 13, 21, 34…). As will be shown below, the progression of the spiral curve maintains the same ratio/proportion rhythm of the Neb (Golden) Proportion. The sides of each golden rectangle maintain the ratio between the sides of each added rectangle to the constant ratio of the Neb (Golden) Proportion (the more things change, the more they stay the same).

Logarithmic spirals are characterized by the golden section properties. A logarithmic spiral is formed by progressive addition by means of "whirling squares" consisting of squares and Neb (Golden) rectangles growing in harmonic progression from center A outward. Each consecutive stage of growth is encompassed by a Neb (Golden) rectangle that is by a square larger than the previous one. In other words, the progression of the Neb (Golden) Proportion yields the whirling squares.

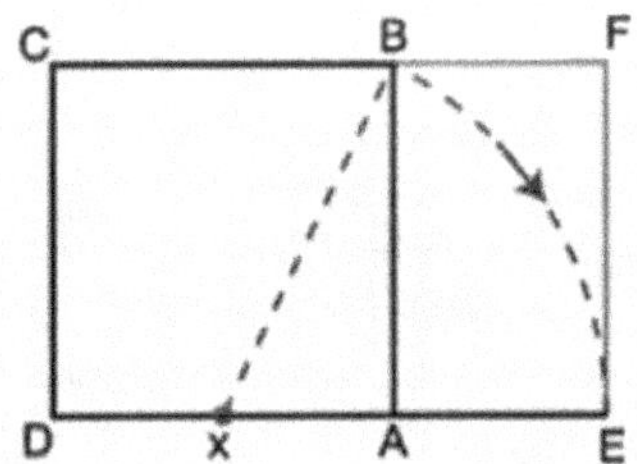

You start with a square ABCD. Then you add the Neb (Golden) rectangle EFBA, as shown above.

- Find the mid-point in DA (i.e. point x).

- Set on point x and draw an arc with a radius of xB, to point E.

- The Neb (Golden) rectangle EFBA is formed.

It should be noted how the two diagonals (DF and BE) are always perpendicular between the smaller and larger Neb (Golden) rectangles. It is therefore that the spiral is called a right angle spiral. It should be noted that the ratio between the two sides (here EF and DE) corresponds with the Golden Proportion (1.618).

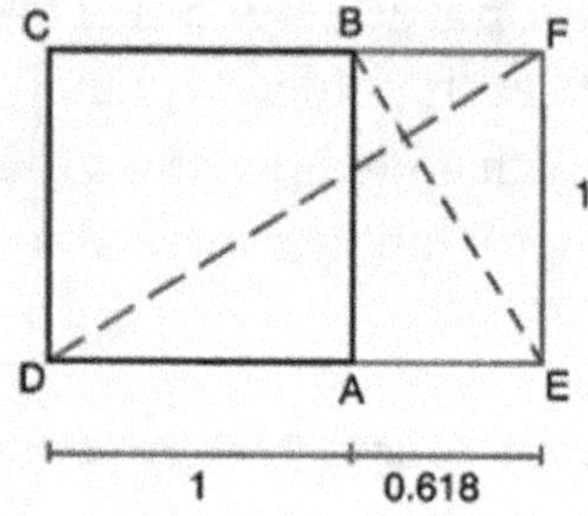

Continue the same process, as indicated below.

squares	+ Neb (Golden) rectangles	= Neb (Golden) rectangles
A B C D	+ E F B A	= E F C D
H E D G	+ E F C D	= H F C G
I J F H	+ H F C G	= I J C G
		= I K L G etc.
J K L C	+ I J C G	

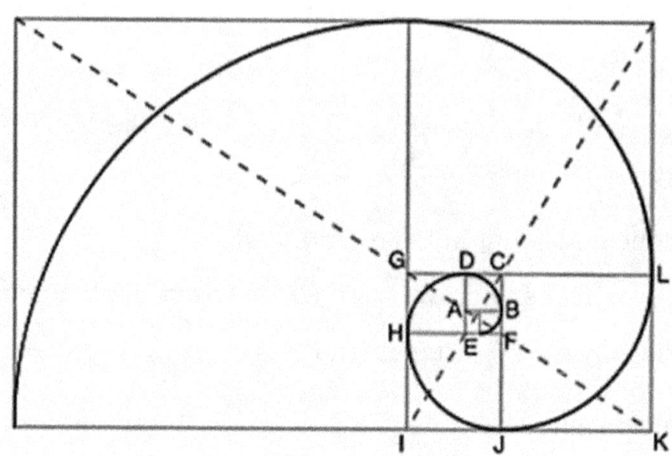

A logarithmic spiral indicated by
"whirling squares"

Since logarithmic spirals follow the same process as the Summation Series, they are subsequently characterized by the Neb (Golden) Proportion. The two dashed diagonals (like all diagonals of the compounded Neb rectangle) are in Neb (Golden) ratio to each other (1.618).

• • •

Logarithmic spirals can also be built by whirling triangles that make use of an isosceles triangle that has a top angle of 36°, i.e. by dividing the circle into 10 divisions.

8.9 DYNAMIC DESIGN APPLICATIONS

The walls of the Egyptian temple were covered with animated images—including hieroglyphs—to facilitate the communication between the above and the below.

The Ancient Egyptian **framework was usually a square**, representing the manifested world **(squaring of the circle)**. Additionally, the square grid itself had the symbolic meaning of the manifested world, which also made it easy to construct the root rectangles of 2, 3, and 5, on/by the square(s) background. The corners of squares and root rectangles were defined by notches along the perimeter or carefully defined by incised lines.

Following are a few examples of the generative dynamic design layout:

i. A simple theme in the square root of two ($\sqrt{2}$) is exhibited in the figure below of the netert (goddess) Nut, the personification of the sky as matrix of all.

The spaces between the bars on either side of the figure were filled with hieroglyphic writing [removed here in order to show the geometric outlines].

   – ABCD is a square.

– The diagonal BD = √2

– Point E was determined so that BE = BD = √2

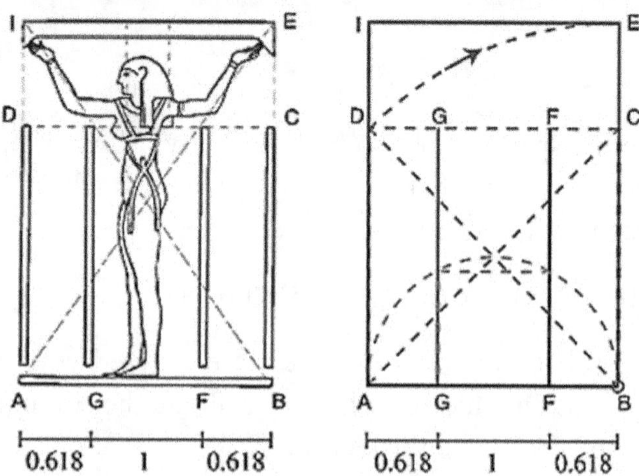

– Lines GG and FF were located based on the principle of inscribing a square into a half circle. [See similar diagram in the next section, ii.]

– The center of action is the hip joint of Nut.

• • •

ii. Here we have a square that is defined by bars cut into the stone at the top and bottom of the composition. The area is dynamically divided for a pictorial composition. The plan of this arrangement is depicted below.

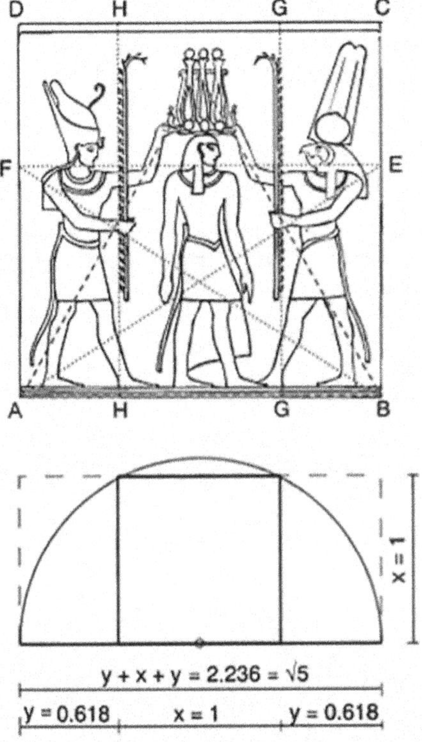

– ABCD is a square.

– A root-five rectangle was used in the center of a square to determine the vertical lines GG and HH.

– The horizontal line EF forms a 5:8 rectangle ABEF.

• • •

iii. The Egyptian bas-relief composition [below] shows that its designer proportioned the picture, as well as the groups of hieroglyphs, by the application of whirling square rectangles to a square. The outlines of the major square are carefully incised into the stone by four bars, two of which have slight pointed projections on either end.

The following are just a few highlights of the design layout:

– ABCD is a square.

– A root-five rectangle was used in the center of a square to determine the vertical lines at points G and H.

– The horizontal line EF forms a 5:8 rectangle ABEF.

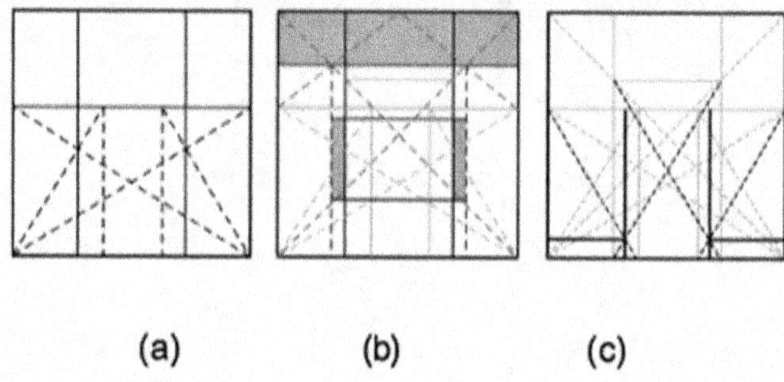

(a)   (b)   (c)

– The general construction plan was that of figure (a) above.

– Spacing for the grouping of the hieroglyphic writing is in figure (b) above.

– Spacing for additional elements of the design is shown in figure (c) above.

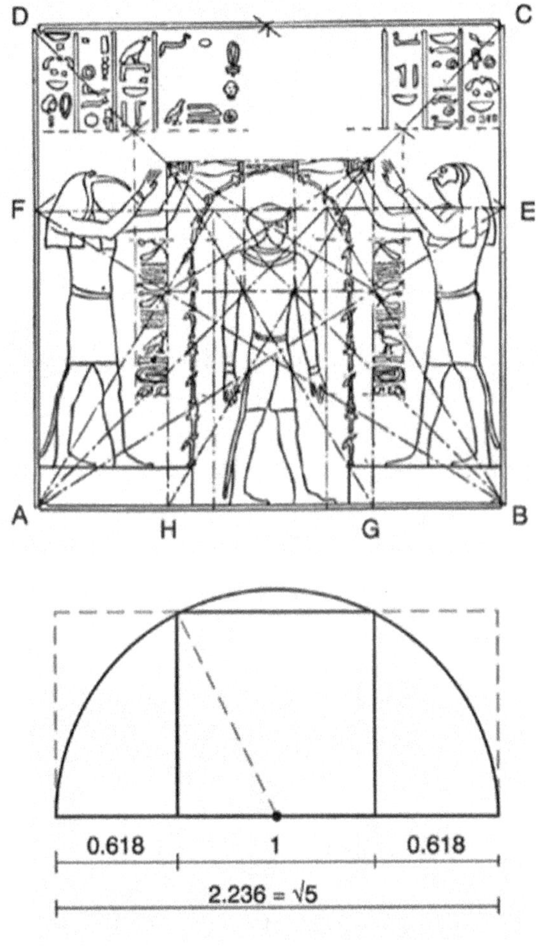

• • •

iv. Generative rectangles in Karnak' Pylon

An interesting observation regarding the significance of the differently proportioned rectangles is found on the pylon at the Temple of Khonsu, at the Karnak Temple Complex.

This pylon shows the falcon, vulture, and ibis, each on a differently proportioned rectangle.

- The falcon of Horus stands on a 1:2 rectangle, which represents the octave—a self-replication.

- The vulture represents Mut, the assimilative power. Therefore, the ratio between the sides of the rectangle is the square root of the Neb (Golden) Proportion. The roots are symbols of pure archetypal, assimilative, generating, and transformative processes.

- The ibis symbol of Thoth is atop a Neb (Golden) rectangle 5:8.

• • •

v. Typical Egyptian Temple Gate:

The typical Ancient Egyptian doorway layout incorporated both sacred ratios (pi and phi), as shown and explained herein.

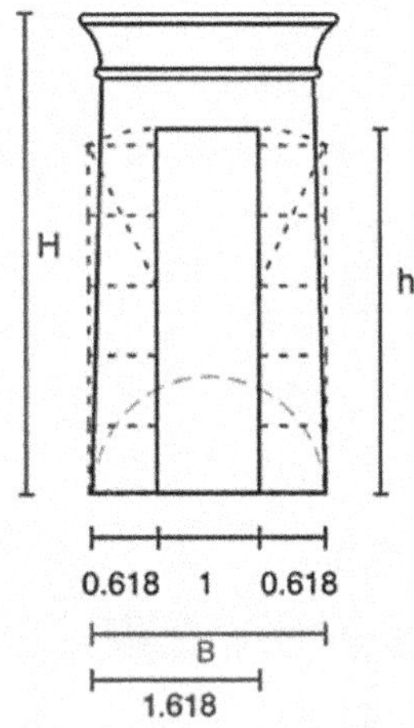

1. The overall outline in the vertical plane is the double-square, 1:2 ratio. [H = 2B]

2. The opening width is based on a square inscribed within a semicircle, the typical Ancient Egyptian way of proportioning a rootfive rectangle. Thus, the thickness of the doorjamb is 0.618 the width of the opening.

3. The height of the aperture (h) = 3.1415 = pi

The incorporation of both sacred ratios [Pi and Phi] in a single unit is found in other Ancient Egyptian works such as the Great Pyramid of Giza. [For more details, read *Egyptian Pyramids Revisited* by Moustafa Gadalla].

• • •

vi. Examples of root rect. in Luxor Temple's Triple sanctuary

The triple sanctuary at the southern extremity of the temple represents the Triple Word, the three-in-one. The separate sanctuaries are symbolic descriptions of the three aspects of the single creative power.

The central chamber is proportioned exactly 8:9; that is to say the ratio of the first musical note of the octave. The sanctuary then "grows" by alternate whole numbers and roots, geometrically expressing the underlying cosmic principle of generation. The root generates the square whose diagonal is in turn the irrational root generating the next square.

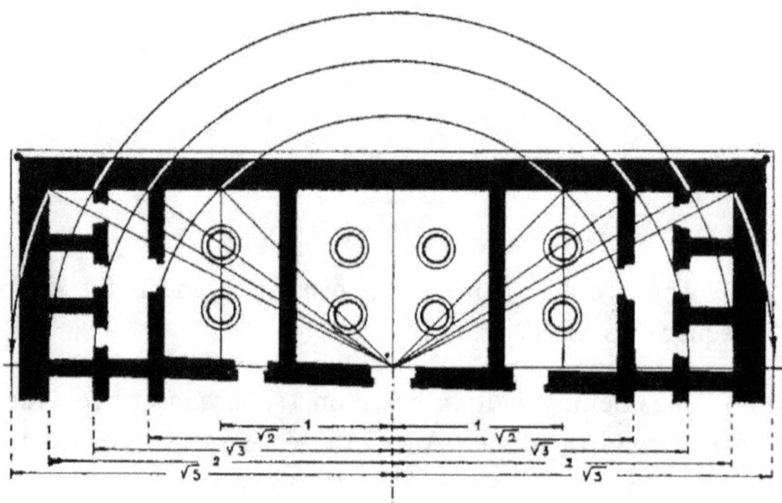

This is a geometric expression of the manner in which creation manifests itself and grows. The temple is therefore a man-made recreation in stone of the metaphysical and cosmic laws of genesis. The temple grows as does the universe.

• • •

More example applications of dynamic design in Ancient Egyptian works are found in Chapter 11 of this book.

Chapter 9 : The Arithmetic Generative Progression

9.1 NUMBER MYSTICISM

In the animated world of Ancient Egypt, numbers did not simply designate quantities but instead were considered to be concrete definitions of energetic formative principles of nature.

For Egyptians, numbers were not just odd and even. These animated numbers in Ancient Egypt were referred to by Plutarch in *Moralia, Vol. V*, when he described the Egyptian 3-4-5 triangle:

> ***The upright, therefore, may be likened to the male, the base to the female, and the hypotenuse to the child of both, and so Osiris may be regarded as the origin, Isis as the recipient, and Horus as perfected result.***

The vitality and the interactions between these numbers shows how they are male and female, active and passive, vertical and horizontal, etc.

All the design elements in Egyptian art and buildings (dimensions, proportions, numbers, etc.) were based on the Egyptian number symbolism.

[For more information about number mysticism read *Egyptian Cosmology: the Animated Universe* by Moustafa Gadalla.]

9.2 THE GENERATIVE NUMBERS

For the Ancient Egyptians, the two primary numbers in the universe are 2 and 3. All phenomena, without exception, are polar in nature and treble in principle. As such, the numbers 2 and 3 are the only primary numbers from which other numbers are derived.

Two symbolizes the power of multiplicity—the female, mutable receptacle – while Three symbolizes the male. This was the music of the spheres—the universal harmonies played out between these two primal male and female universal symbols of Osiris and Isis, whose heavenly marriage produced the child Horus. Plutarch confirmed this Egyptian knowledge in *Moralia, Vol. V*:

> ***Three (Osiris) is the first perfect odd number: four is a square whose side is the even number two (Isis); but five (Horus) is in some ways like to its father, and in some ways like to its mother, being made up of three and two...***

The significance of the two primary numbers 2 and 3 (as represented by Isis and Osiris) was made very clear byDiodorus of Sicily [*Book I*, 11. 5]:

> ***These two neteru*** (gods), ***they hold, regulate the entire universe, giving both nourishment and increase to all things...***

9.3 PROGRESSION OF GROWTH AND PROPORTION

The sequence of numerical creation of Isis followed by Osiris followed by Horus is 2, 3, 5, . . .

It is a progressive series where you start with the two primary numbers in the Ancient Egyptian system, i.e. 2 and 3. Then you add their total to the preceding number, and on and on—any figure is the sum of the two preceding ones. The series would therefore be:

2

3

5 (3 + 2)
8 (5 + 3)
13 (8 + 5)
21 (13 + 8)
34 (21 + 13)
55 (34 + 21)
89, 144, 233, 377, 610, . . .

The Summation Series is reflected throughout nature. The number of seeds in a sunflower, the petals of any flower, the arrangement of pine cones, the growth of a nautilus shell, etc.—all follow the same pattern of these series.

Since this Series was in existence before Fibonacci (born in 1179 CE), it should not bear his name. Fibonacci himself and his Western commentators did not even claim that it was his "creation". Let us call it as it is—a Summation Series.

The Summation Series conforms perfectly with (and can be regarded as an expression of) Egyptian mathematics, which has been defined by everyone as an essentially additive procedure. This additive process is obvious in their reduction of multiplication and division into the same process: by breaking up higher multiples into a sum of consecutive duplications. It involves a process of doubling and adding. This progressive doubling lends itself to speedy calculation. It is significant that the methods used in modern calculators and computers are closely related to the Egyptian method.

The overwhelming evidence indicates that the Summation Series was known to the Ancient Egyptians. Many Ancient Egyptian plans of temples and tombs throughout the history of Ancient Egypt show along their longitudinal axis and transversely dimensions in cubits (one cubit =1.72' (0.523 m), giving in clear and consecutive terms the Summation Series 2, 3, 5, 8, 13, 21, 34, 55, 89, 144, 233, 377, 610 . . .

There has been evidence about the knowledge of the Summation Series ever since the Pyramid (erroneously known as mortuary) Temple of Khafra (Chephren) at Giza, built in 2500 BCE about 3700 years before Fibonacci.

The essential points of the temple [shown below] comply with the Summation Series, which reaches the figure of 233 cubits in its total length, as measured from the pyramid, with TEN consecutive numbers of the series.

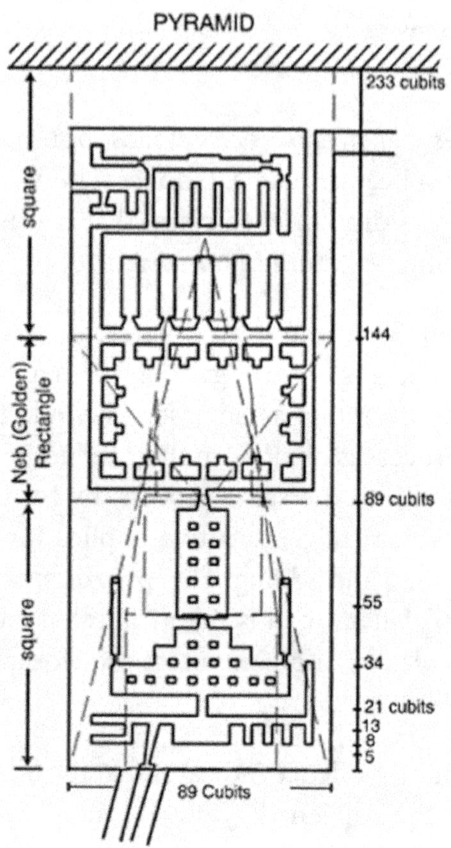

9.4 THE SUMMATION SERIES AND THE GOLDEN PROPORTION

This series was the origin of Ancient Egyptian harmonic design.

It offers the true pulsation of natural growth. The ratio between each group of two consecutive numbers follows the pulsation:

3:2 = 1.5
5:3 = 1.667
8:5 = 1.60
13:8 = 1.625
21:13 = 1.615
34:21 = 1.619
55:34 = 1.618
89:55 = 1.618
144:89 = 1.618, . . .

So, as the series progresses, the ratio between successive numbers tends towards the Neb (Golden) Proportion (which numerically = 1.618), to which Western academia has recently assigned an arbitrary symbol—the Greek alphabet letter ϕ (phi) – even though it was known and used long before the Greeks. This proportion is also known in Western texts as 'Golden' and 'Divine'.

Western academia has even misrepresented the Neb (Golden) Proportion by calling it the *Golden Number*. A proportion is not a number, it is a relationship. 'Number' implies the capacity to enumerate.

The term 'Golden Section' did not come into use in Western texts until the 19th century. In most Western mathematical books and journals, the common symbol for the Neb (Golden) Proportion is tau (τ) instead of phi (ϕ)—presumably because tau is the initial letter of the Greek word for *section*.

The Neb (Golden) Proportion controls the proportions of innumerable living organisms which are manifested in the logarithmic/equal angle spirals.

9.5 THE COSMIC PROPORTION OF THE HUMAN FIGURE

Proportion is the commensuration of the various constituent parts with the whole. The human body is a prime example of such harmonic proportion, where the human frame has been formed with such propriety that the several members are commensurate with the whole.

The Ancient Egyptian canon for the harmonic proportion of human figures differed only between children and adults. The differences were reflective of the actual physical differences at these two stages. At birth, it is the navel that divides the height of child into two halves. Upon maturation (reaching puberty), the junction of both legs (reproductive organs) is at mid-height of the adult figure. The position of the navel now divides the height into unequal parts that make the parts and the whole in compliance with the Neb (Golden) Proportion.

The oldest discovered records from the 5th Dynasty show that the highest defined point along the vertical axis is the hairline of the person's head, when presented in the earthly realm.

Egyptian figurations carefully mark—with a headband, crown, diadem, or joint—a dividing line for the top of the skull of the earthly man, thus separating the crown of the skull. The height of the body was measured exclusive of the crown, as shown herein in this recovered Ancient Egyptian grid.

The representation of the neteru (gods/goddesses) and/or human beings in the afterlife are shown on an 18-square grid, for the full height to the top of the head (i.e. including the crown of the head).

The difference in the height between the two realms reflects the Ancient Egyptian's deep understanding of the physiology and role of humans on Earth.

The removal of this part of the human brain (the crown of the head) leaves man alive but without discernment, hence with no personal judgment. The person is in a vegetative state, living and acting only as the executant of an impulse that he receives, without actual choice. It is like a person in a coma.

The navel is located about 11.1 grid squares from the bottom of the heel on the 18-square grid system (or the same equivalent ratio 0.618 for grid or non-grid systems). Such division follows the laws of harmony between the two parts themselves, and the parts to the whole, as per the following two relationships:

1. The ratio between the Two (top and lower) Parts of the divine height (18 grid squares) are harmonic.

Top : Lower is 0.618
Lower : Top is 1.618

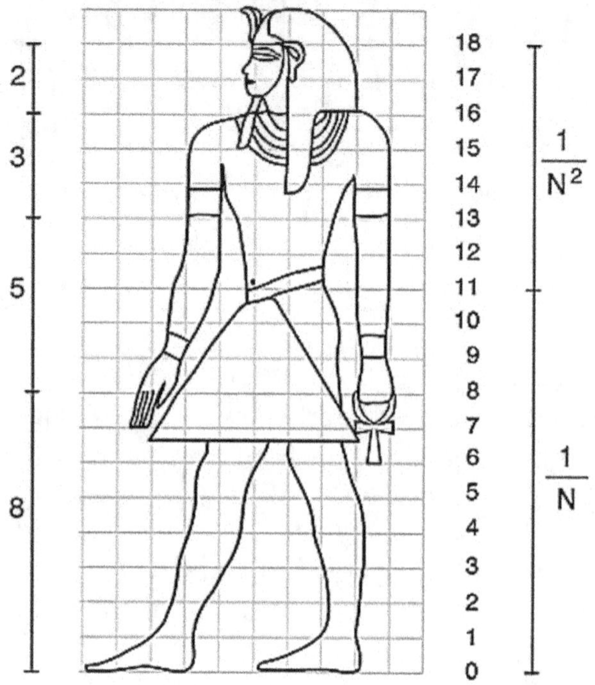

2. Between the Two Parts to the whole Unity (divine height)—taking the full height (to the hairline of the earthly man's head) as 1—the body from the feet to the navel, in the Egyptian canon, is equal to the reciprocal of the Neb (Golden) Proportion (1/N), i.e. 0.618. The portion from the navel to the hairline of the head equals the power 2 of the reciprocal of the Neb (Golden) Proportion (1/N2), or 0.382.

$$1 / N + 1 / N^2 = 1$$
$$0.618 + 0.382 = 1$$

where N = the Neb (Golden) Proportion (1.618)

Because of the intimate relationship between the Summation Series and the Neb (Golden) proportion, we find that the different parts of the figure also follow the Summation

Series [as depicted in the above original grid from KV22 of Amenhotep III].

More about mathematics in Ancient Egypt in the appendices section of this book.

Chapter 10 :
Combined—Arithmetic and Graphic Harmonic Design of Egyptian Buildings

10.1 THE HARMONIC DESIGN PARAMETERS

Harmonic design in Ancient Egyptian architecture was achieved through a unification of two systems:

1. Arithmetic (significant numbers).

2. Graphic (square, rectangles, and a few triangles).

The union of the two systems reflects the relationship of the parts to the whole, which is the essence of harmonic design.

This union of arithmetic and graphic design follows the elements described below.

1. The Arithmetic System Consisted of:

<u>**1-a. The Active Axes**</u>

An axis is an imaginary and ideal line about which a moving body revolves. In geometry, an axis is equally imaginary—a line without thickness.

The Egyptian temple was regarded as an organic, living unity. It is in constant motion; its intricate alignments and its multiple asymmetries make it oscillate about its axes. This movement takes place within a rhythm given by the "module" or the particular coefficient of the thing or idea to be defined.

Ancient Egyptian architectural design is conspicuous for its strong apparent symmetry around a longitudinal axis. This is the result of the Ancient Egyptian knowledge of cosmic laws. The Egyptian designer reflected such slight cosmic asymmetry by ensuring that elements on either side of the axis are not exactly identical to one another. While most of them are balanced, elements are not symmetrical.

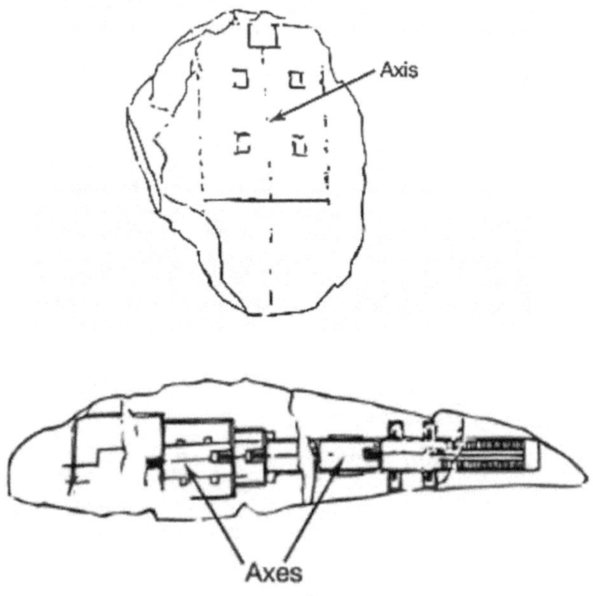

The axis line can be found in a few recovered architectural drawings or sketches on papyri and tablets from various periods. They were, presumably, workmen's notations, and in spite of their practical purpose, they still feature the axis line drawn in the same conventional way as in modern drawings.

In the buildings themselves, the axis is marked by an engraved line on the stones of the upper course of a foundation slab, such as the case at Luxor Temple.

<u>**1-b. Significant Points (Along the Axis)**</u>

Significant points were determined along the design axis. These points mark the intersection with transverse axes, the alignment of a central doorway, the position of an altar, the center of the sanctuary, etc. These significant points follow a precise arithmetic progression. In many of the best plans, these significant points are at harmonic distances from one another, and their distances from one end to the other express the figures of the Summation (so-called Fibonacci) Series, 3, 5, 8, 13, 21, 34, 55, 89, 144, 233, 377, 610, . . . The harmonic analysis shows a series of significant points readable from both ends, i.e. if inverted, a system of significant points would also correspond to the Series with the reference point starting at the opposite end of the plan.

High numbers of the Summation Series were crystallized in the Egyptian monuments ever since the Old Kingdom. The design of the pyramid temple of Khafra (Chephren) reaches the figure of 233 cubits in its total length, as measured from the pyramid, with a complete series of TEN significant points.

The Karnak Temple follows the Summation Series' figures up to 610 cubits, i.e. TWELVE significant points. [See diagrams of both temples in the next chapter].

2. The Graphic System Consisted of:

<u>**2-a. The Telescopic Triangles**</u>

The typical Egyptian temple plan increases in width and height from the sanctuary towards the front. This over-all delimitation was based upon a "telescopic system" of design since the Old Kingdom. The increase in width was accomplished by the use of consecutive 1:2, 1:4, and 1:8 triangles from one or more significant point(s). [See diagram of Karnak Temple (partial) below.]

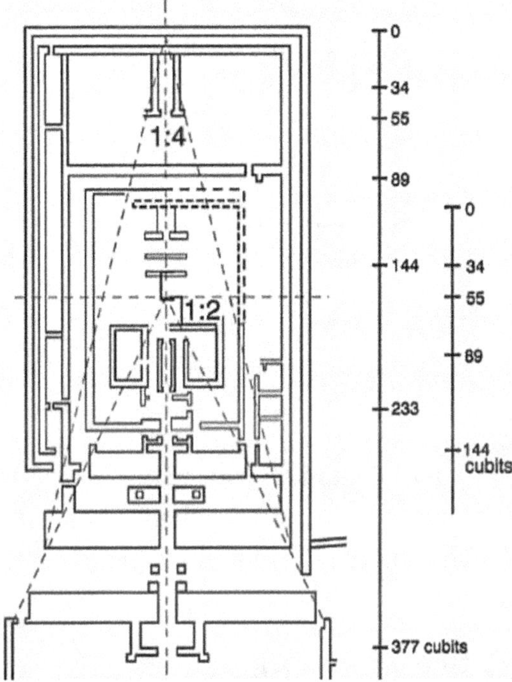

The same telescopic configuration applied to the vertical plan, whereby the floor of the temple descended and the roofs ascended outwardly towards the temple's pylons; as shown in several temples in an earlier chapter of this book.

2-b. The Rectangular Perimeters

The general horizontal and vertical outlines are basically rectangular in shape, for the overall plan as well as its constituent parts. The most common configurations that were used are:

- A simple square, such as that utilized in the Pyramid Temple of Khafra (Chephren) in Giza.

- A double square or 1:2 rectangle, such as the Zoser Complex at Saqqara, the inner enclosure at Karnak, and the festival hall of Twt Homosis III

- Root Rectangles—numerous examples [shown below].

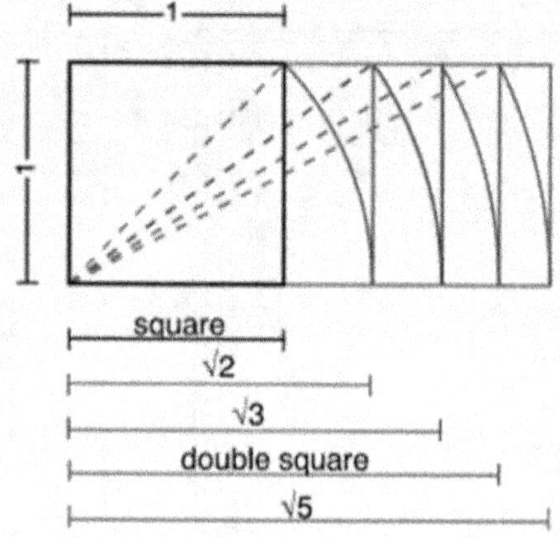

- The Neb (Golden) Rectangle, where the "numerical value" of the ratio between the two sides equals 1.618—numerous examples such as in the Pyramid Temple of Khafra in Giza [shown earlier].

10.2 THE VERTICAL PLANE

The Ancient Egyptians were masters of the vertical principle as well as the horizontal line. Vertical heights followed the same proportional increase as horizontal widths as additions were made to the front of monuments—an aspect characteristic of the Egyptian temples.

Harmonic proportion was applied by the Ancient Egyptians in all three dimensions, such as:

- The pyramids (square bases and triangle volume).

- The striking case of the King's Room in Khufu (Cheops) Pyramid, which affords exact relations for the great diagonal in space with respect to the dimension of the side. [See diagram in Chapter 11.]

- Pylons. [See diagram in Chapter 11.]

- Doorways/portals/gates. [See diagram in Chapter 11.]

- Vertical heights followed the same proportional increase as horizontal widths, as additions were made to the front of monuments—an aspect characteristic of the Egyptian temples.

Various applications of harmonic design in Ancient Egyptian works throughout its recovered history—and throughout the land—are found in the next chapter of this book.

Chapter 11 : Harmonic Analysis of Ancient Egyptian Works

11.1 GENERAL

The Ancient Egyptians manifested their knowledge in harmonic proportion long before its pre-dynastic era, continuing throughout its dynastic history. The selected diagrams shown in this chapter are just a few examples, spread along Egypt's long-known history. Please note:

1. The diagrams are based on measurements by various and independent sources [see Sources & Notes for each specific reference].

2. In order not to overwhelm the reader with crowded drawings and columns, many details of the Ancient Egyptian buildings are not shown on the following diagrams. Simpler layout drawings will make it easier for the reader to see the consistent application of harmonic proportion in Egyptian works.

3. In some cases, distances shown in these diagrams were converted into Egyptian cubits so that the Ancient Egyptian knowledge and consistent use of the Summation (so-called Fibonacci) Series becomes very clear.

4. Of the example buildings used in this chapter (and the entire book), none of them have been touched during for-

eign rule, so there is not the slightest doubt that Egyptians had this knowledge long before any foreigners ever set a foot in Egypt.

11.2 PRE-DYNASTIC ERA (5000-2575 BCE)

Because of the remote age of the pre-dynastic era, only mastaba-type tombs survived in the remote areas of Egypt. The superstructure of the mastaba tombs, even during the pre-dynastic era, followed harmonic proportions, as evident in tombs in the Abydos, Memphis, and Giza areas.

A large number of Egyptian mastabas were documented by Aug. Mariette's general catalogue of the monuments of Abydos, Paris 1880. Mariette found about 800 of them during his excavations at Abydos.

Most of the simplest tombs conformed to the 5:8 Neb (Golden) rectangle.

Several tombs were composed of a combination of a square and a 5:8 Neb (Golden) rectangle.

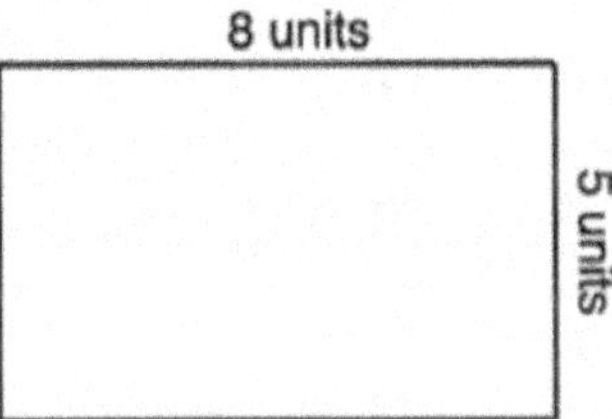

To have hundreds of tombs throughout the country with such harmonic proportion shows that it was common knowledge, even at that early age.

• • •

Since temples require restoration every few decades/centuries, we find that every temple in Egypt includes references that they were built in pre-dynastic times. As such, temples from various dynastic eras are generally restorations of pre-dynastic works.

11.3 OLD KINGDOM (2575-2150 BCE)

Mastaba Tombs

In order to show that harmonic proportion was common knowledge, here are a few examples of mastaba-type tombs in Giza. The rectangular superstructures are oriented north-south, and show harmonic designs, as shown below.

– Mastaba Tomb 6 (Giza)

The constructional diagram consists of a square and a 5:8 Neb (Golden) rectangle.

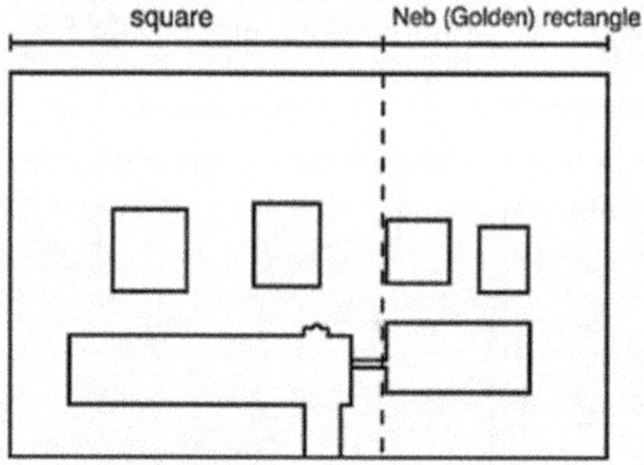

Most other tombs are a simple 5:8 Neb (Golden) rectangle, as per the indicated measurements:

– Mastaba Tomb 86 (Giza): 12.6' (3.85 m) x 20.1' (6.17 m)

– Mastaba Tomb 87 (Giza): 19.1' (5.82 m) x 31.2' (9.52 m)

– Mastaba Tomb 105 (Giza): 9.7' (2.95 m) x 15.6' (4.75 m)

Khufu (Cheops) Pyramid's Granite Room

Khufu's pyramid is located in Giza, and was built during his reign (2551-2528 BCE). The floor plan of the room is a double square (2 x 1 rectangle), 20 x 10 Egyptian cubits (34'-4" x 17'-2", 10.5 x 5.2 m).

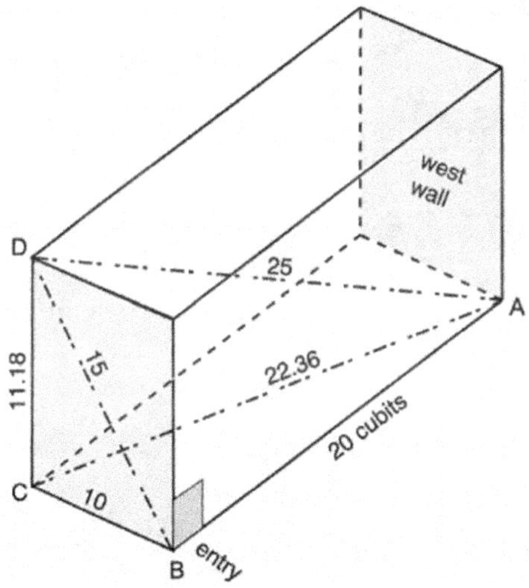

The double square, divided by a single diagonal CA, forms two right triangles, each having a base of 1 and a height of 2. The diagonal CA is equal to the square root of 5 (2.236), i.e. 22.36 cubits in actual length.

The height of the room is designed to be one half the length of the floor diagonal CA, i.e. $\sqrt{5}/2$, which is 11.18 cubits (19'-2" or 5.8 m) in actual length.

This choice of CD, as the height of the room, will make the diagonal DB (in the triangle DCB) equal to 15 cubits. The result is that the three sides of the triangle ABD are in relation of 3:4:5.

The harmonic proportion of this room shows the intimate relationship between 1:2:3:4:5 and demonstrates the relationship in the divine harmonic proportion (sacred geometry) between process and structure. It also shows that the right-angle triangle principle (so-called Pythagoras) was practiced in Egyptian design regularly, 2,000 years before Pythagoras walked this earth.

• • •

A complete analysis of the interior and exterior of masonry pyramids in Egypt is detailed in *Egyptian Pyramids Revisited* by Moustafa Gadalla.

Pyramid Temple of Khafra

This temple was built during Khafra's (Chephren) reign (2520-2494 BCE), and is located in Giza next to his pyramid. Points of interesting harmonic proportion in this massive, yet very exact structure include:

1. The almost symmetrical plan.

2. It consists of two squares connected by a 5:8 Neb (Golden) rectangle.

3. All significant points [explained in earlier chapter] are clearly connected, even to the corners of the massive piers.

4. The significant points along the longitudinal axis correspond to the numbers of the Summation (so-called Fibonacci) Series [3, 5, 8, 13, 21, 34, 55, **89**, 144, **233**, 377, 610,…]. The total length to the pyramid is **233** cubits, while the width is **89** cubits.

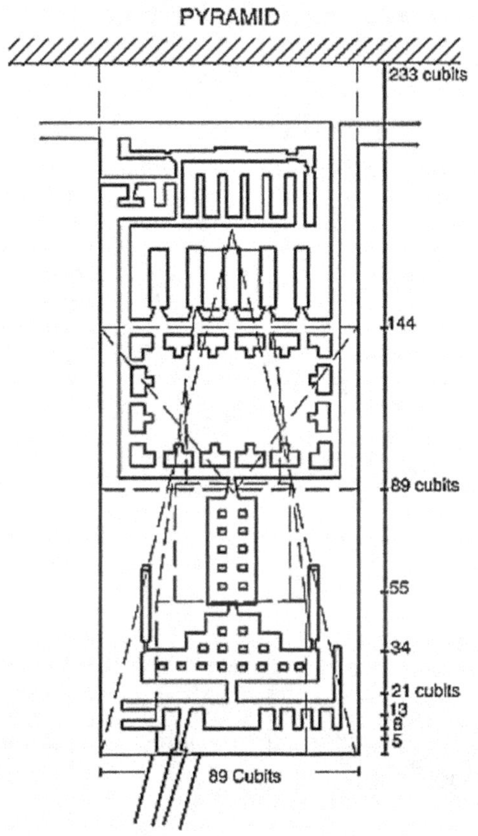

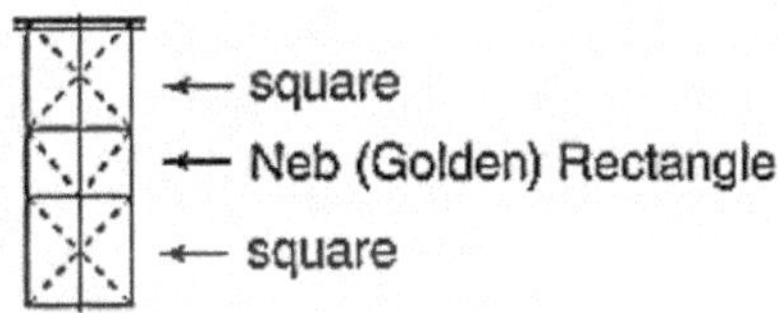

Menkaura's (Mycerinus) Pyramid

This is the last masonry pyramid built during the Pyramid Age. This pyramid is the smallest and youngest of the three pyramids on the Giza Plateau. It was built by Menkaura (2494-2472 BCE), and has the following interesting harmonic design characteristics:

1. The base is a perfect square with four triangular-shaped surfaces in space.

2. Its cross section is very nearly a 5:8 triangle, representing the Neb (Golden) triangle.

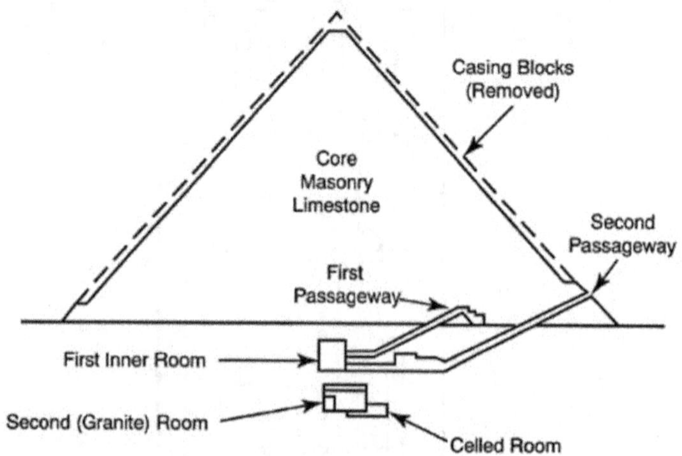

3. The ratio of the height to half the diagonal is 8:9 (the perfect musical tone).

Menkaura's pyramid represents the perfect harmony for sight and sound.

This pyramid signified the end of the Pyramid Age.

• • •

A complete analysis of the interior and exterior of masonry pyramids in Egypt is detailed in *Egyptian Pyramids Revisited* by Moustafa Gadalla.

11.4 MIDDLE KINGDOM (2040-1783 BCE)

<u>**Peripteral Chapel Of Sen-usert (Sesostris) I**</u>

The pavilion of Sen-usert I (1971-1926 BCE), at the Karnak Temple Complex, incorporates geodesic knowledge in its design, and it also provides a wealth of geodesic information on its walls. It has a list of all the provinces of Egypt with their respective land surface areas, proving that actual surveys were made. Major towns are listed, the total length of Egypt is given, and the normal height of the Nile flood at three principal points along the length of the river is noted. Much additional useful information is also provided on these walls.

The constructional diagram is a square flanked by a 5:8 Neb (Golden) rectangle on each side, delimiting the length of both stairways.

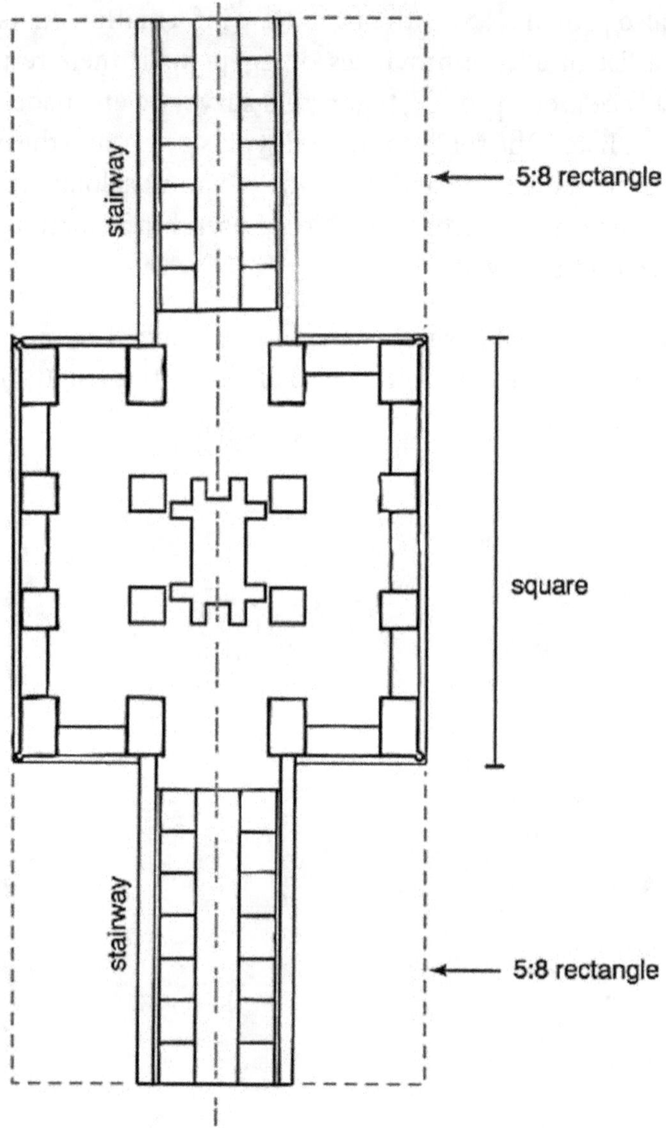

Tomb of Wahka

Wakha's rock-cut tomb was constructed ca. 1900 BCE at Qaw near Asyut, and is partly cut into the cliff. The layout is terraced,

featuring a pillared portico, sloping causeway, stairway, courtyard, and superimposed columned porticos.

Points of interesting harmonic proportions include:

1. The upper part of the complex, stretching on many levels,
consists of squares connected by a scissors-like lattice of 5:8
Neb (Golden) triangles/rectangles.

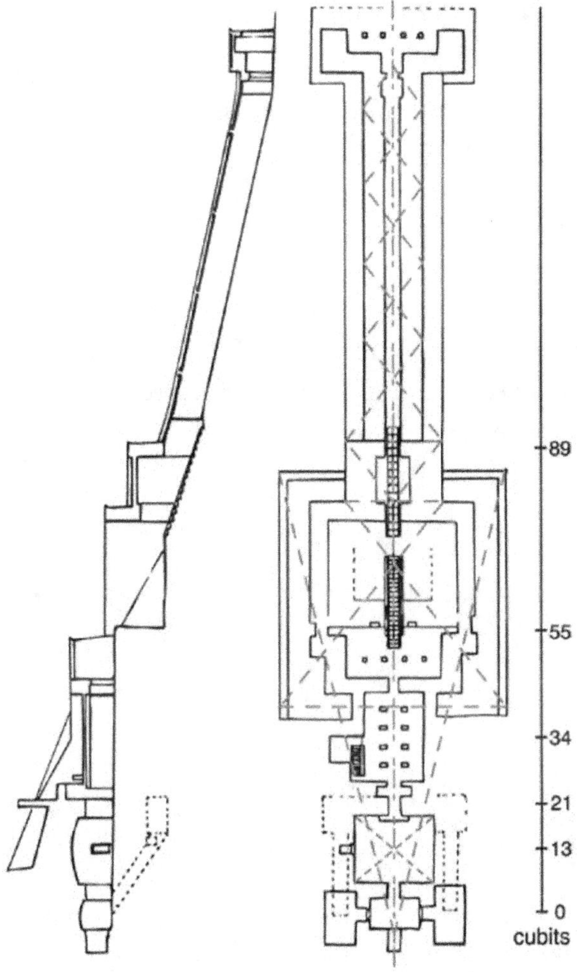

2. The complex, excluding the front stairway, is propor-

tioned based on five numbers of the Summation (Fibonacci) Series.

This example shows that far away from the populated centers of Memphis and Thebes, harmonic proportion was common knowledge throughout the country.

11.5 NEW KINGDOM (1550-1070 BCE)

Karnak Temple Complex

The original sanctuary of the Karnak Complex at Luxor (Thebes) was built during the Middle Kingdom. This is the largest complex of temples in Egypt, where the temples, pylons, courts, columns and reliefs were continually added to from the Middle to the Late Kingdom for over 1,500 years.

Although dating from various periods, the temples comply with the principles of harmonic design. This is important evidence to support the existence of archives where records of the projects were kept for reference.

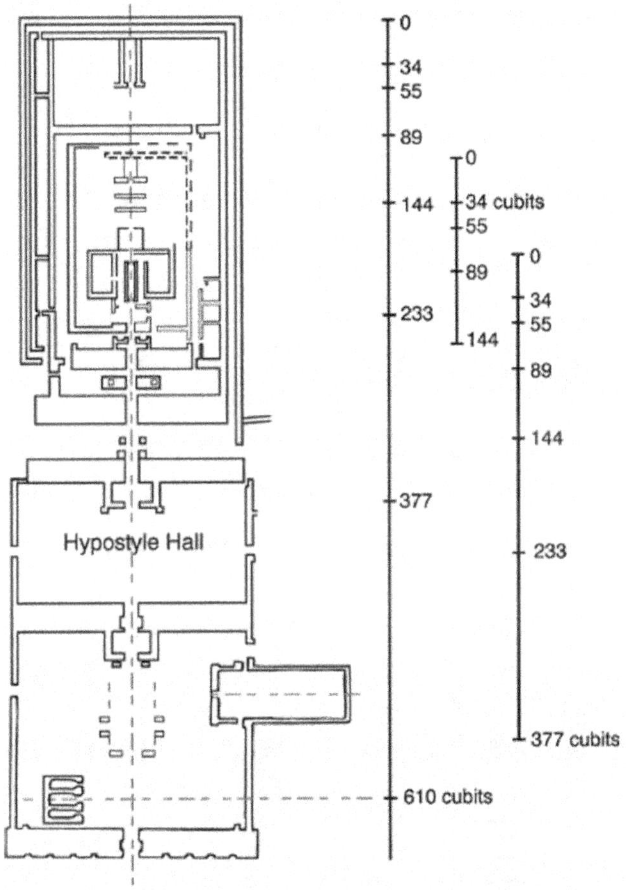

This is a good example of a temple constructed by accretion through successive additions.

If we consider only the main axis (west-east) temple, we will find that more than one Summation (Fibonacci) Series [3, 5, 8, 13, 21, 34, 55, 89, 144, 233, 377, **610**, …] of significant points shows the application of comprehensive harmonic design along three different scales. The greatest distance is **610** cubits from the external rear to the axis of the triple shrine, in the front courtyard.

Osiris Temple at Abydos

This well-preserved temple at Abydos has an unusual L-shaped plan. This work is dated to Seti I (1333–1304 BCE) and was completed by Ramses II (1304–1237 BCE).

Points of interesting harmonic proportion include:

1. The harmonic design took into account the shift of the lateral part of the L-shape. The basic scheme is continuous throughout the main body and lateral part of the plan.

The temple outline plan consists of a square topped with three 5:8 Neb (Golden) rectangles and the rear lateral section is one 5:8 Neb (Golden) rectangle of the same width as the main portion.

2. A series of significant points are determined in the main body, beginning at the rear wall of the sanctuaries. The distances coincide with the numbers of the Summation (so-called Fibonacci) Series [3, 5, 8, 13, 21, 34, 55, 89, 144, 233, 377, 610,...] up to 233 cubits, which determines the front alignment of the two enclosures in the forecourt.

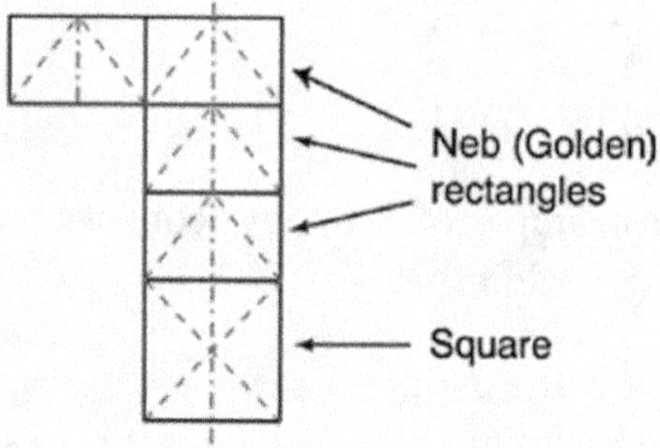

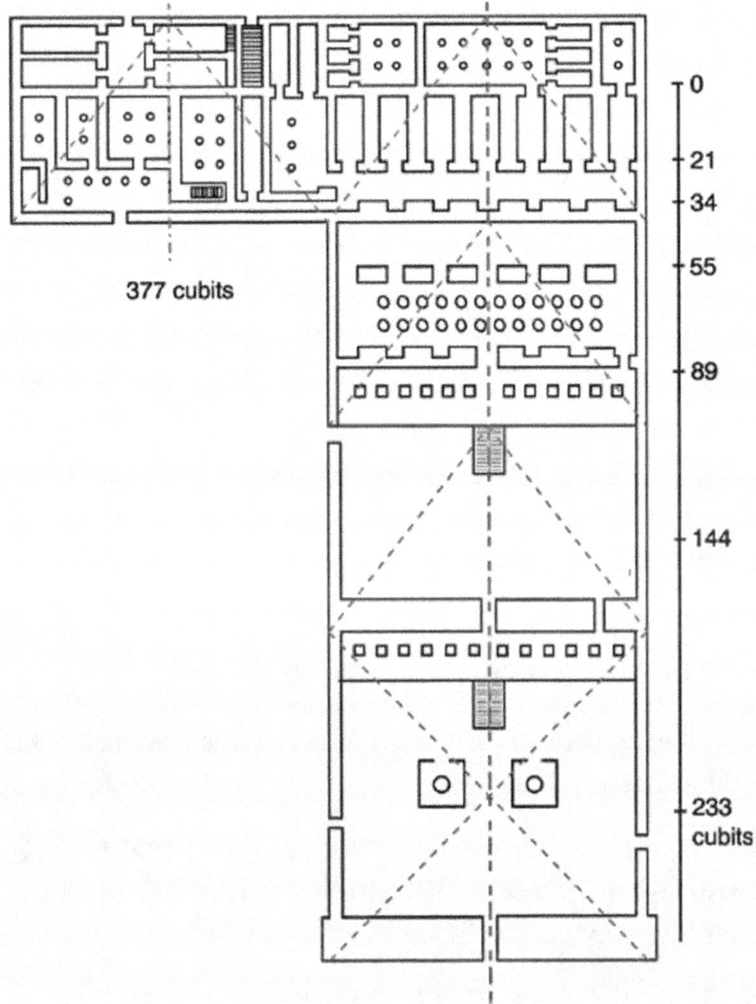

It is noteworthy that the subsequent number of the series, 377, determines the total length of the temple if the lateral portion of the L-shape is stretched out to the axis of the outer gateway opening on to the lateral part.

Tomb of Ramses IV

The tomb of King Ramses IV (1163–1156 BCE) in the Valley of Kings at Luxor (Thebes) has the following interesting harmonic features:

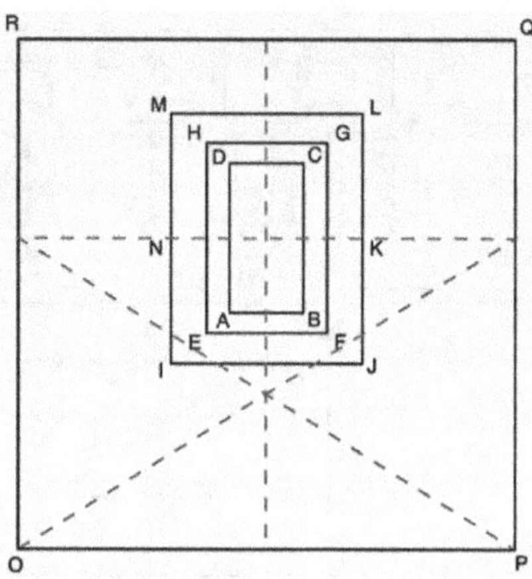

1. The tomb OPQR contains a triple sarcophagus. The tomb itself was dimensioned on a projection of the geometry of this triple sarcophagus.

2. The innermost sarcophagus ABCD is in the form of a double square—the holiest of sacred enclosures.

3. The middle sarcophagus EFGH is in the form of a 5:8 Neb (Golden) rectangle.

4. The outer sarcophagus IJLM has two 5:8 Neb (Golden) rectangles IJKN and NKLM each of which is equal to the middle sarcophagus EFGH.

11.6 THE LAST NATIVE EGYPTIAN PHARAOH

<u>Khnum Temple</u>

This temple was erected by the last Egyptian Pharaoh, Nectanebo II (360-343 BCE) at Elephantine, and was enlarged during the Ptolemaic and Roman era. The temple shows that even at the end of Egypt's dynastic history, the general layout followed a well-defined harmonic scheme. The temple has points of interesting harmonic proportion, such as:

1. Prior to the Ptolemaic era, the temple's width was estab-

lished as **55** cubits at its rear. The length was extended during the reign of Egyptian Nectanebo II to **89** cubits, with 8 significant points corresponding to the numbers of the Summation (Fibonacci) Series. Then later during the Ptolemaic rule, the row of columns in the vestibule was built at the **89** cubit length so that the scheme of the harmonic diagram is a square **89** topped with a 5:8 Neb (Golden) rectangle. With the later additions of a rear enclosure, forecourt, and pylon, the total length amounts to **233** cubits, with an intermediate significant point evident at **144** cubits from the rear end to the alignment of the forecourt before its final arrangement.

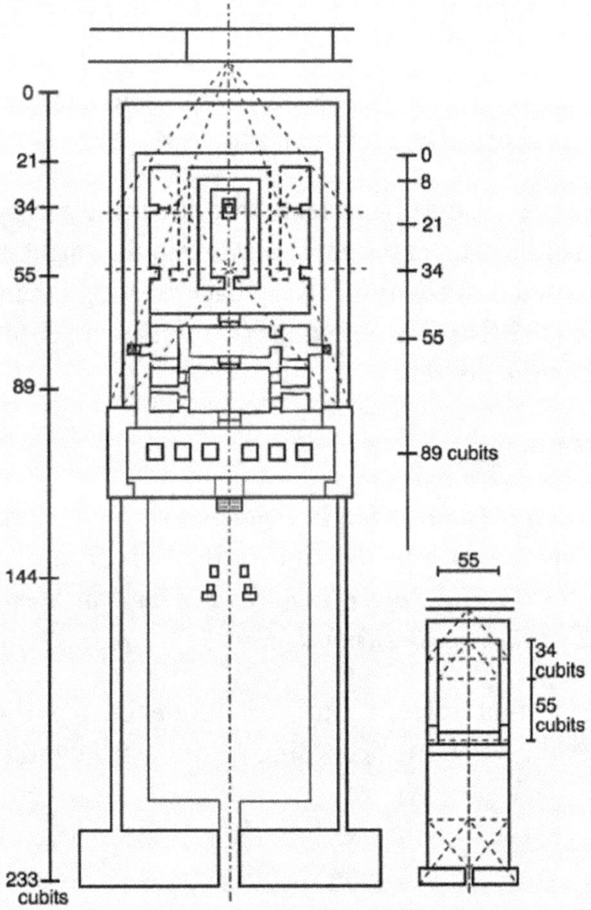

2. All the above critical distances (such as **55, 89, 144, and 233)** are clearly numbers from the Summation (so-called Fibonacci) Series [3, 5, 8, 13, 21, 34, **55, 89, 144, 233,** 377, 610 …].

3. This shows that temple construction in ancient Egypt, even during foreigners' presence, was based on purely ancient Egyptian design criteria (as is obvious in the earlier works in Ancient Egypt) and was subsequently copied by others.

11.7 RESTORATIONS DURING GRECO-ROMAN PERIOD (332 BCE – 395 CE)

Several Ancient Egyptian temples were restored during the Greco-Roman period. The restored temples show consistent compliance with the Egyptian canon of proportion that has been utilized for the prior several thousand years.

A clear example comes from texts inscribed in the crypts of the temple of Hathor at Dendera which was rebuilt during the Ptolemaic Era based on drawings dating back to King Pepi of the 6th Dynasty (2400 BCE). The drawings themselves are copies of pre-dynastic documents.

The text reads:

> *The venerable foundation in Dendera was found in early writings, written on a leather roll in the time of the Servants of Horus (= the kings preceding Mena/Menes), at Memphis, in a casket, at the time of the lord of the Two Lands... Pepi.*

It is evident that restoration work done during the Greco-Roman period was done according to Ancient Egyptian knowledge.

11.8 MISCELLANEOUS ITEMS

General

Harmonic design was not restricted to the large ancient Egyptian architectural buildings, but was used in the smaller structures and elements such as capitals and stelae, as well as in graphic compositions and statuary which are all constituent parts of the whole building.

The pectorals and other magic amulets found on mummified Egyptians have been geometrically analyzed. They all show various configurations of harmonic proportion, which demonstrates the unity of Egyptian sacred geometry from the largest to the smallest sacred object.

We shall present a few examples of smaller (relatively speaking) items, such as:

- Capitals of Columns
- Stelae
- Pylons
- Doorways/Gateways

Capitals of Columns

The design of capitals in Ancient Egypt was based on 1:2, 1:4, and 5:8 Neb (Golden) triangles. The following are three types of Egyptian-designed capitals:

1. The **papyriform** capital—from Ramses III Commemorative Temple (Medinat Habu), western Luxor. The diameter of the capital is twice that of the shaft or abacus. A 5:8 Neb (Golden) triangle defines the proportions between the widest edge of the corolla, acting as a base, and the third of the five binding rings.

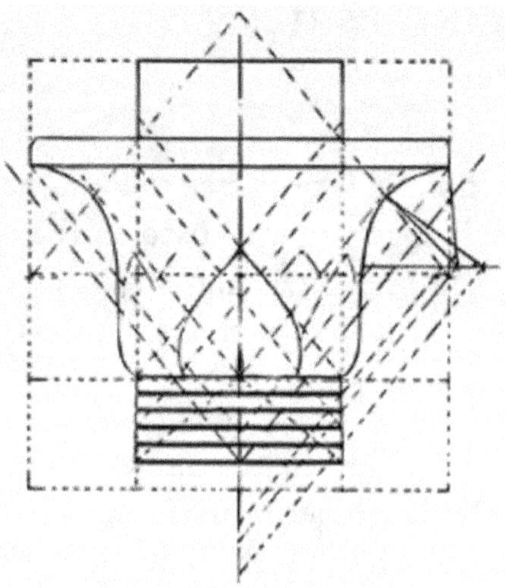

2. The **lotiform** or papyriform bud capital—Karnak Temple (ca. 1335 BCE). The constructional diagram for the outline features a square, derived proportionally from the diameter of the shaft by means of a 5:8 Neb (Golden) triangle and giving the height of the trapezoidal cross section of the bud. The widths at the top and bottom of the bud are determined by two 5:8 triangles. It is noteworthy that the decorations of the five rings and the stylized vertical stems beneath have a square outline.

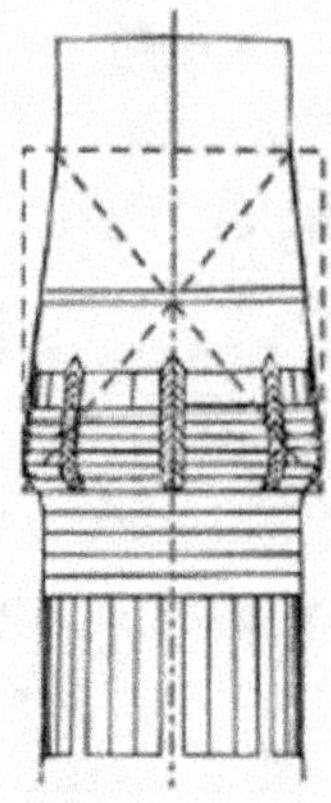

3. The peculiar inverted **campaniform** capital of the tent-pole column in the festival hall of Tuthomosis III

(1490-1436 BCE) at Karnak has its height determined by the height of the 5:8 triangle whose base equals the largest diameter of the corolla.

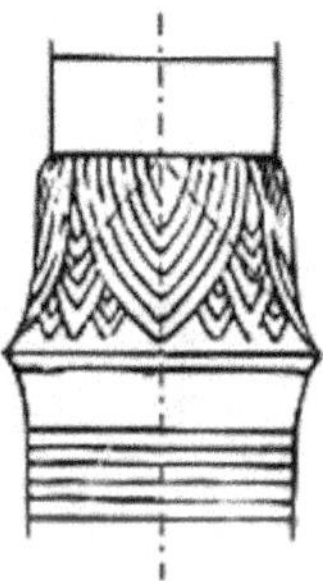

<u>Stelae</u>

Egyptian stelae from different eras were designed according to well defined harmonic proportions. Examples of the internal panel configurations are:

1. Stela of King Watchi at Abydos, 1st Dynasty (ca. 3100 BCE).
A square topped with a 5:8 Neb (Golden) triangle.

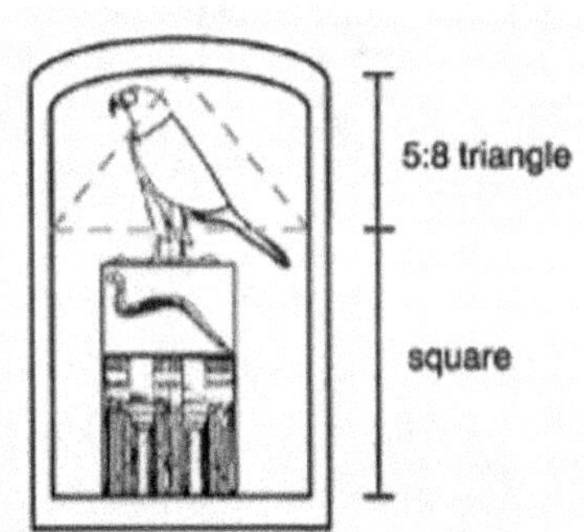

2. Stela 20088 at Cairo Museum, Middle Kingdom (2040-1783 BCE)
Twin squares.

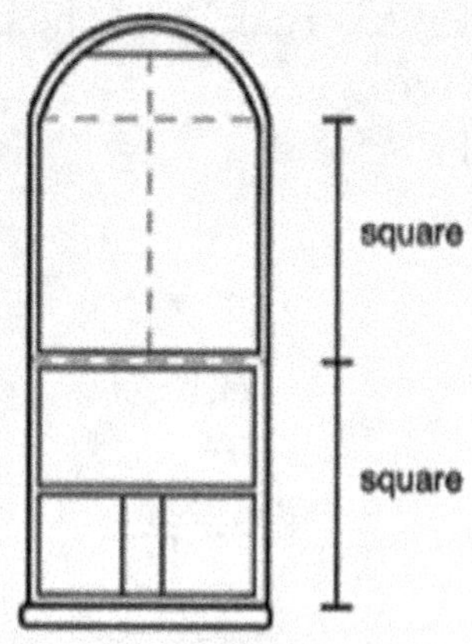

3. Stela 20255 at Cairo Museum, Middle Kingdom. Twin 5:8 Neb (Golden) rectangles.

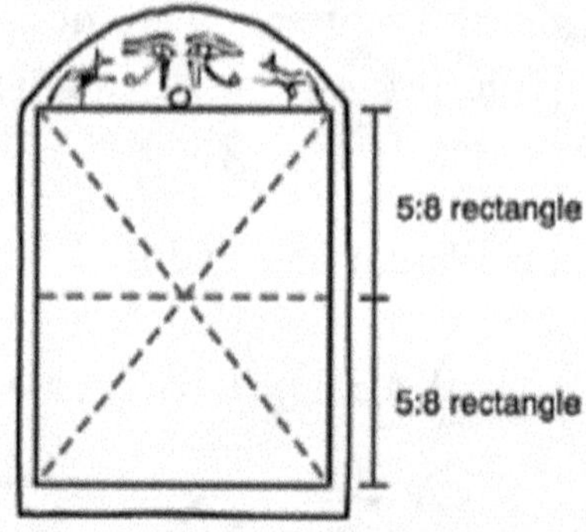

Pylons

Pylons are a permanent feature of Egyptian temples. An example of the harmonic proportion of an Egyptian pylon is located at the Temple of Khonsu (ca. 1330 BCE) at the Karnak Temple Complex. The unique harmonic proportion of this 19th Dynasty pylon was noted in *The Description of Egypt* [Part III, page 57], written during Napoleon's time.

The whole width is divided into three parts: M + m + M. The portal takes up the middle part of the width, and there are pylon towers arising on both sides of the portal.

Whole width = B
Whole height = H
Width of the Pylon-Tower = M
Width of the portal/gate = m
Opening of the gate, height = h
Opening of the gate, width = b

Points of interest in the harmonic proportion are:

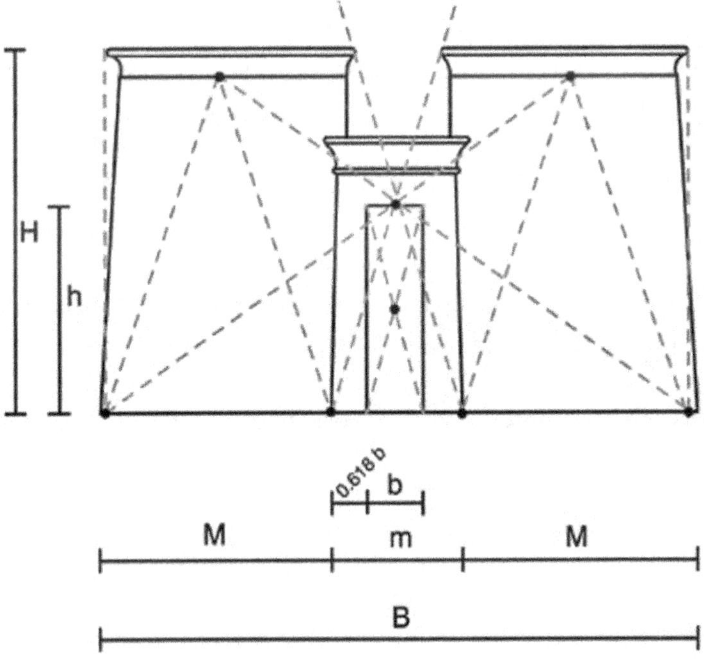

1. The ratio of total width to total height (B/H) = 1.618. That means that the pylon forms a vertical Neb (Golden) rectangle.

2. M/m = 1.618, i.e. the ratio of the width of the pylon to the width of the portal is the Neb (Golden) proportion.

3. Each pylon-tower is a golden rectangle in the vertical plane (H/M = 1.618)

4. The relationships between B, H, M, and m are:

B x 0.618 = H
B x 0.6182 = M
B x 0.6183 = m

Doorways/Gateways

In Ancient Egypt, doorways were built with or without a pylon on each side.

A few examples from different periods show that the simple design of Egyptian doorways conforms to a harmonic analysis. The relationships between the openings and the doorjambs were harmonically proportioned. The height of the aperture and the full height were also harmonically designed.

Points of interesting harmonic proportions are:

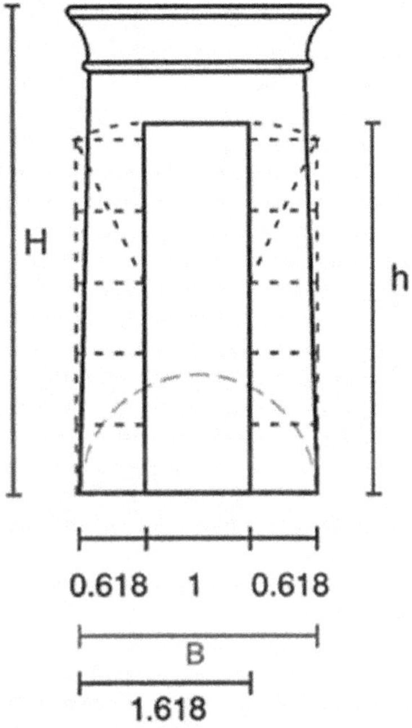

1. The overall outline in the vertical plane is the double-square, 1:2 ratio [H=2B]

2. The opening width is based on a square inscribed within a semi-circle, the typical Ancient Egyptian way of proportioning a root-five rectangle. Thus, the thickness of the door-jamb is 0.618 the width of the opening.

3. The height of the aperture (h) = 3.1415 = pi

The typical Ancient Egyptian doorway layout incorporated both sacred ratios pi and phi, as shown and explained above.

The incorporation of both sacred ratios was intentionally utilized 4,500 years ago in the construction of the masonary pyramids of Egypt. [For details, read *Egyptian Pyramids Revisited* by Moustafa Gadalla.]

PART III : THE SPIRITED COMMUNICATIONS

Chapter 12 : The Animated Metaphysical Images on Walls

12.1 THE ACTIVE DYNAMIC DESIGN

As we have shown above, Ancient Egyptian temples were meant to generate energies and were designed accordingly and built according to active dynamic design principles. We have also shown the overall telescopic configuration of the Egyptian temple with jointing patterns in order to ensure the flow of energies.

We have also shown the Egyptian application of dynamic design on the configuration and layout of the 'symbolic' characters of depictions on the walls of Egyptian tombs and temples.

In this chapter, our focus will be on the metaphysical meanings of such depictions.

The walls of the Egyptian temple were covered with animated images—including hieroglyphs—to facilitate the communication between the micro cosmos and the macro cosmos. The inscriptions and illustrations on the temple walls have deep mystical meanings known only to certain enlightened people. The carvings were of ritualistic value.

12.2 THE PICTORIAL IMAGES' METAPHYSICAL SIGNIFICANCE

A picture is worth a 1,000 words—and by extension, several

thousands of sounds. A picture represents a concept/idea and not a single letter/sound.

We say "picture this" or "imagine that", for images are representations of concepts and ideas beyond words. The picture conveys information more efficiently than letters/words.

Pictorial images are the (metaphysical) language of the mind/intellect/divine.

Human beings process information received from the five senses to the brain through visualized images. As such, pictorial images represent scientific/metaphysical realities as the ultimate medium for the human consciousness that interprets, processes and maintains the meanings of such images.

Modern science concurs that a series of images are processed in the consciousness the same way as dream processing.

[For detailed information about this subject, read *The Egyptian Hieroglyph Metaphysical Language*, by Moustafa Gadalla.]

12.3 THE WEALTH OF KNOWLEDGE IN THE EGYPTIAN PICTORIAL FORMATIONS

A symbol, by definition, is not what it represents, but what it stands for; what it suggests. A symbol reveals to the mind a reality other than itself. Words convey information; symbols evoke understanding.

A chosen symbol represents that function or principle on all levels simultaneously, from the simplest, most obvious physical manifestation of that function to the most abstract and metaphysical. Without recognizing the simple fact about the intent of symbolism, we will continue to be ignorant of the wealth of Egyptian knowledge and wisdom.

In Egyptian symbolism, the precise role of the Egyptian

ideograms was revealed in many ways: by dress, headdress, crowns, feathers, animal, plant, color, position, size, gesture, sacred object, or type of symbolic equipment (e.g., flail, scepter, staff, ankh).

Symbolism is reflected in form, size, location, materials, color, number, etc.

This symbolic language represents a wealth of physical, physiological, psychological, and spiritual data in the symbols/signs.

Man's depiction signifies The Universe—The Divine and Earthly Realms

So many phrases are being used throughout the world which consistently state that the human being is made in the image of God (i.e. a miniature universe); and that to understand the universe is to understand oneself and vice versa. Yet, no culture has ever practiced the above principle like the Ancient Egyptians. Central to their complete understanding of the universe was the knowledge that man was made in the image of God and, as such, man represented the image of all creation.

Consistent with such thinking, a depicted human being represents both the universe as a whole as well as the human being on Earth. The difference between the two will be explained below.

As stated earlier, the oldest discovered records from the 5th Dynasty show that the highest defined point along the vertical axis is the hairline of the person's head, when presented in the earthly realm.

Egyptian figurations carefully mark—with a headband, crown, diadem, or joint—a dividing line for the top of the skull of the earthly man, thus separating the crown of the skull. The height of the body was measured exclusive of the crown. The illustrations show the earthly man as always higher than the divine aspects.

A clear example is found here in this Ancient Egyptian papyrus with a grid system, where a human is higher than the neter (god) Thoth.

It should be noted that the depicted neter (god) Thoth illustrates both the vertical (18-grid squares) and the horizontal stretched arm-span (fathom) measuring 22-square grid.

The representation of the neteru (gods/goddesses) and/or human beings in the afterlife are shown on an 18-square grid for the full height to the top of the head. The choice of the number 18 is very significant and is consistent with all other Ancient Egyptian aspects. In the *Unas Funerary* (so-called *Pyramid*) *Texts*, the Divine Man (King) is generated from 2 x 9, (i.e. 18) divine units:

> **The King** [symbol of the Divine Man]**came forth from between the thighs of the two divine Nines.**

The difference in the height between the two realms reflects the Ancient Egyptian's deep understanding of the physiology and role of humans on earth.

The removal of this part of the human brain leaves man alive, but without discernment; hence with no personal judgment. The person is in a vegetated state, living and acting only as the executant of an impulse that he receives, without actual choice. It is like a person in a coma.

The earthly being must use his cerebral instrument to choose his actions. These actions will be in agreement or at variance with natural harmony. If, during his/her earthly life, the actions are not harmonious with nature, s/he will reincarnate again to the earthly realm, to try another time.

When earthly man has developed his consciousness to the utmost perfection, he will no longer need his cerebral instrument.

Animal Symbolism

The Egyptians' careful observation and profound knowledge of the natural world enabled them to identify certain animals with specific qualities that could symbolize certain divine functions and principles in a particularly pure and striking fashion.

When we talk about loyalty, there is no better way to express loyalty than with a dog.

When we talk about the protective aspect of motherhood, there is no better way to express it than with a lioness.

This symbolic expression of deep spiritual understanding was presented in three main forms. The first and second are animal-headed humans, or a pure animal form.

The third form is the opposite of an animal-headed human. In this case, we have a human-headed bird—that is the Ba—representing the body soul hovering over the body.

The depiction of the Ba, then, is the divine aspect of the terrestrial.

Animal Headed Images

An animal-headed human figure/image represents a particular function/attribute in its purest form. When an animal-headed figure/image is presented, it conveys that particular function/attribute in the universe—being depicted in human form—consistent with the theme that man is the image of the whole creation. Animal-headed human images represent the divine forces which the Egyptian called Neteru (gods, goddesses). They are manifestations of the divine energy in the universe.

[For more details about the cosmic functions of the neteru (gods, goddesses), read other publications by same author, especially *Egyptian Cosmology* and *Egyptian Divinities*.]

Accessories, Emblems, Color, etc.

In Egyptian symbolism, the precise role of the neteru (gods/goddesses) are revealed in many ways: by dress, headdress, crown, feather, animal, plant, color, position, size, gesture, sacred object (e.g., flail, scepter, staff, ankh), etc. This symbolic language represents a wealth of physical, physiological, psychological, and spiritual data in the presented symbols.

Action Forms—Body Language

The careful definition of the separate planes of this cubic universe is revealed in an art which is essentially two-dimensional. In order to represent three-dimensional objects on a plane surface, the Egyptians avoided the perspectival solution of the problem. That resulted in a two-dimensional profile with the exception of a few parts of the body, like the eyes and sometimes the horns.

Practically all figures on the walls of the Egyptian buildings are in profile form, indicative of action and interaction between the various symbolic figures. A wide variety of actions in the forms are evident.

One must view these depictions in the proper perspective—how does this series of depictions relate to each other; but first, how do these depictions fit in the overall picture, being in context?

As stated earlier, the Egyptians proportioned the pictorial figures, as well as the hieroglyphs, by the application of generative dynamic design.

The pictorial depiction both in hieroglyphs and figurative images are presented in animated, precise active modes.

One may describe it as a form of body language.

   1. The immobile figure, a still profile, where the vertical axis passes through the ear (inner ear, equilibrium), hip joint, and ends in the heel of the foot.

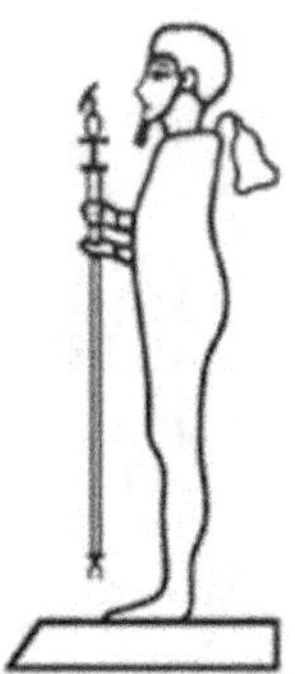

   2. The same as #1, except that both shoulders are shown, with a front view of the chest indicative of restricted action.

3. Same as #2, except that one foot is positioned slightly ahead of the other—the beginning of movement.

4. The figure is in motion (the normal stride), when the axis of movement passes from the ear (balance) to the hip joint and ends at the ball of the rear foot. It is on the ball of the foot that one places one's weight in order to move forward.

5. The running figure (the long stride), as shown on this original Ancient Egyptian grid of the Bird Catcher, remi-

niscent of Papageno, in Mozart's Masonic Opera *The Magic Flute*.

6. The action of working together.

7. Sitting broad-shouldered, in an active mode.

8. Leaning.

9. Kneeling and leaning.

10. The dancing girl, a four-step animated motion.

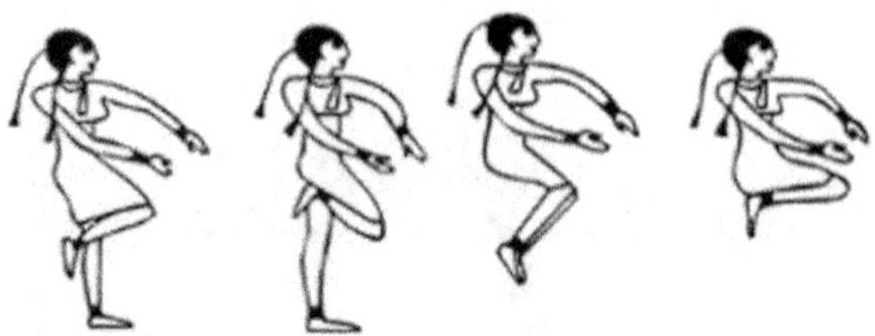

12.4 METAPHYSICAL MEANINGS OF SOME DEPICTIONS

In viewing the tombs and temples, it is worth repeating the point that, for Ancient Egyptians, every 'physical' aspect of life had a symbolic (metaphysical) meaning. But also, every symbolic act of expression had a 'material' background. As above so below, and vice versa.

The familiar Egyptian scenes of daily life activities are never seen in the tomb of the king. The scenes of daily activities are portrayed in the tombs of nobles and high officials.

The scenes of daily activities, found inside Egyptian tombs, show a strong perpetual correlation between the Earth and heavens. The scenes provide graphical representations of all sorts of activities: hunting, fishing, agriculture, law courts, and all kinds of arts and crafts. Portraying these daily activities in the presence of the neteru (gods, goddesses) or with their assistance signifies their cosmic correspondence—a strong perpetual correlation between the Earth and heavens.

This perpetual correlation—cosmic consciousness—was echoed in Asleptus III [25] of the *Hermetic Texts*:

> **...in Egypt all the operations of the powers which rule and work in heaven have been transferred to earth below...it should rather be said that the whole cosmos dwells in [Egypt] as in its sanctuary...**

Every action, no matter how mundane, had in some sense a cosmic corresponding act: plowing, sowing, reaping, brewing, the sizing of a beer mug, building ships, waging wars, playing games. All were viewed as earthly symbols for divine activities. In other words, to Ancient (and Baladi) Egyptians, every 'physical' aspect of life had a symbolic (metaphysical) meaning. But also, every symbolic act of expression had a 'material' background.

The following are a few examples of the metaphysical meanings of earthly physical activities, as portrayed in the wall scenes in Ancient Egyptian tombs:

> 1. The typical Egyptian tomb sowing and reaping scene parallels the biblical parable, **"Whatsoever a man soweth, that shall he also reap"**. This was intended to be a spiritual message, not agricultural advice.

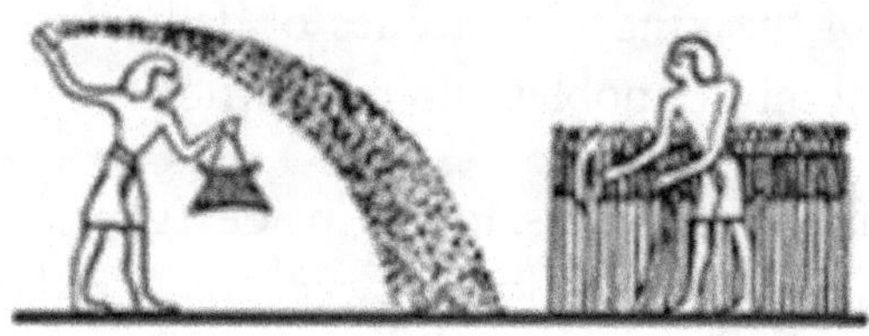

2. Cause and Effect: Both Horus and Thoth are shown in numerous illustrations in the Ancient Egyptian temples, performing the symbolic Uniting of the Two Lands. Horus represents

conscience, mind,and intellect, and is identified with the heart. Thoth represents manifestation and deliverance, and is identified with the tongue. One thinks with the heart and acts with the tongue.

3. Spiritualization of Wine: The wine-making process of growing, harvesting, pressing, and fermenting is a metaphor for spiritual processes which can be equated to the biblical wine symbolism.

The walls of the Ancient Egyptian tombs show vintners

pressing new wine [as per the Ancient Egyptian tomb scene shown above], and wine-making is everywhere as a constant metaphor of spiritual processes and the themes of transformation and inner power.

The soul, or the portion of god within, causes divine ferment in the body of life. It's developed there, as on the vine, by the sun of man's spiritual self. The fermented potency of wine was, at its deepest spiritual level, a symbol of the presence of the incarnated god within the spiritually aware person.

4. Odor of Sanctity: A woman/man sniffing at the lotus is a recurrent theme in Egyptian tombs. The perfume of the lotus is its spiritualized essence, similar to the "odor of sanctity" in Christian

traditions. The depiction of the lotus is very common in Egyptian symbology.

5. Playing Games—People of all classes and the neteru (gods/goddesses) are depicted on Ancient Egyptian tombs and temples as playing all types of games. Such games included board games as well as physical activities and sporting events.

Ancient and classical writers affirmed that games owe their development, if not their very origin, to religious observances. Many accounts of games are mentioned by Homer as essential to the accompaniment of devotional ceremonies.

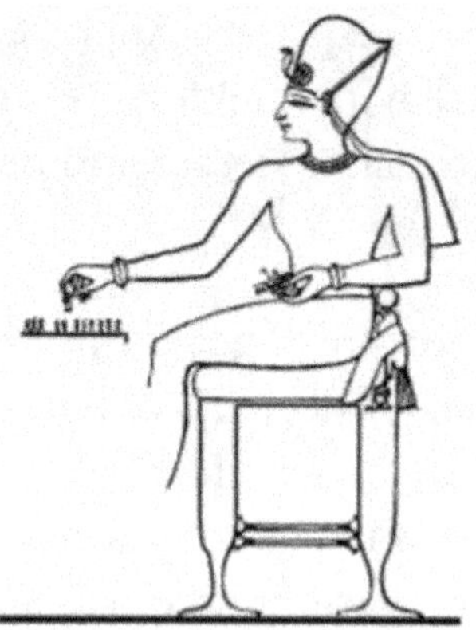

Ramses III, playing at draughts.
His tomb in Ta-Apet (Thebes).

Playing at mora.   Playing at odd and even.
From tombs in Ta-Apet (Thebes)

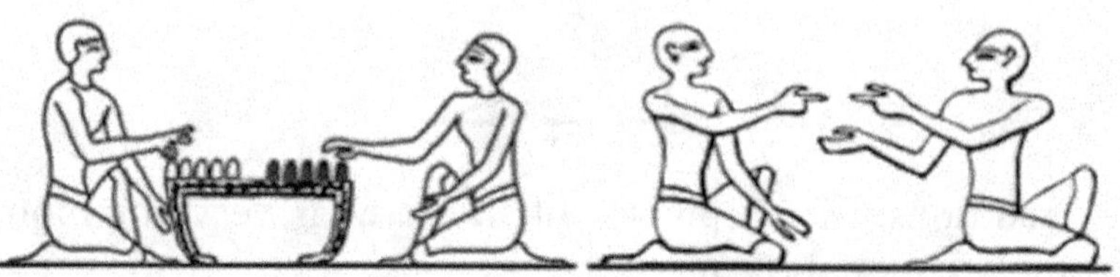

Playing at draughts.   Playing at mora.
From Beni Hassan tombs

The numerous Egyptian festivals include all types of games
and activities that are an essential part of the festivities, and
are as much a part of the festival as the religious processions
and the visits to the holy shrines.

6. The bird-netting scene and the various species of birds
depicted on walls have specific metaphysical significance. In
general, these wild birds represent "wild" spiritual elements

that must be trapped, caged, sometimes tamed, or offered to the neteru (gods/goddesses) in sacrifice.

A modern similarity in symbolism is found in Mozart's Masonic opera *The Magic Flute*, where Papageno is the free spirit whose specialty is trapping wild birds.

7. Fishing scenes are plentiful in Egyptian temples and tombs. In the Egyptian texts, Heru (Horus) assumes the form of a fisherman and his four disciples ("sons") also fish with him.

Fishing scene from a tomb at **Ta-Apet** (Thebes). The right side shows the fishermen trapping the fish. The left shows a boat with the fish hanging up to dry in the sun and wind.

Christ used a similar symbolism by making his disciples fishers of men.

8. King, subduing the forces—the scene on the outer walls

of the temple and the walls of the outer courtyard show the battle of the forces of light (represented by the king) subduing the forces of darkness (represented by the foreign enemies). The same scene is repeated at temples throughout the country, which signifies its symbolism and is never a representation of actual historical events.

9. Hands symbolism—the hand hand symbolized/symbolizes several concepts; one of which is action, and therefore of creation and latent creative power.

An active right hand symbolizes giving. An active left hand signifies receiving.

When the symbolic role of the person is wholly active, he is shown with two right hands. When his role is wholly passive, such as when he is receiving the gift of life from the neteru (gods, goddesses), he has two left hands.

Chapter 13 : Human Activities

13.1 TEMPLE ORGANIZATION

The temple was a self-contained holy city that combined the functions of the medieval cathedral with the functions of all the guilds.

The temple priesthood consisted of various grades, such as the chief priests or pontiffs; the prophets; sacred and royal scribes; and other support staff such as dressers or keepers of the sacred robes; the bearers of the shrines, banners, and other holy emblems; draftsmen; masons; and embalmers. Various other officers were in charge of processions and other religious ceremonies.

The elaborate temple services required a variety of offerings. These provisions came from nearby workshops and kitchens.

Kitchens and bakeries began their activity at dawn to prepare the day's offering of breads, cakes, and sacrificial beef and fowl.

13.2 STARTUP ACTIVATION OF IMAGES

The Egyptian artist presented, in his work, the idea of objects rather than their exact realization in a spatial context. Their creative artistic concept is similar to God's creative actions. As a result of God's Word (utterance), the world was created. Similarly, every creative work of art, even a statue, has inscriptions describing the action or defining its purpose as well as the names of the actors.

Additionally, each statue, painting, relief, or building had to undergo, upon its completion, the ritual of the *Opening of the Mouth* to ensure that it was transformed from an inanimate product of man's hands into a vibrant part of the divine order charged with numinous power.

13.3 REGULAR TEMPLE RITUALS

As the interface between the divine and human spheres, the pharaoh and the priests who functioned as his appointed agents performed ritual services at the temple. In return, the neteru (gods, goddesses) gave life to the land and upheld Egypt's ordained place in the cosmos. In one sense, the Egyptian temple was the source of power by which all of Egyptian society ran.

The Egyptian temple had its own distinctive rituals. The most prominent aspect of the Egyptian rituals was the presentation of material offerings: bread, beer, rolls of linen, meat, fowl, and other goods. The offerings symbolize the man's success in transforming raw matters into finished products-bread, beer, linen, etc. The Egyptian view was that all mundane activities were resonant of the cosmic process of transforming raw matters into perfected creations.

The offerings are made to the neteru (gods, goddesses) who originally transformed the chaos of the primeval waters into the orderly world of creation. Ceremonies were performed throughout the day. There were two main services, in the morning and evening. Offerings were prepared at dawn in the kitchens and bakeries.

The priests, meanwhile, purified themselves in the waters of the sacred lake outside the temple. The priests entered the temple and performed further purification in the temple's outer corridors. They then led a long procession of offering-bearers, incense bearers, and a chorus of singers chanting hymns of praise. The procession proceeded deeper into the temple as a priest opened the successive doors one by one, up to the sealed sanctuary. The offerings were then laid out on tables and altars and the offering-bearers withdrew.

The high priest then entered the sanctuary, which included its sacred ark and a little shrine of granite or basalt. The shrine contained the image of the neter. The priest held the effigy of the neter and then prayed towards each of the four cardinal directions. The platter of symbolic offerings was then presented.

A short while later, other offerings were made to the subsidiary deities of the temple.

The effigy was then washed and dressed again, in brand new fine linen. It was then anointed with precious ointment and placed back in the shrine.

The rituals of washing and dressing the effigy of the neter were based upon and coordinated with the movements of the stars in heaven. Because these movements were the result of divine cosmic law, the rituals showed that Egypt was always attuned to the eternally-unfolding rhythms of the universe. The priest sprinkled the shrine with holy water and gave offerings of sacred resins and salts to the neter. He then veiled the effigy again, sealed the shrine, and retraced his way back out of the temple.

A relatively short service was observed at noon. The evening service was longer. It was, however, the morning celebration that manifested the victorious spirit of light over darkness.

13.4 THE TEMPLE'S COURT OF THE MULTITUDE

The outer court was often accessible to the common people, at least in part or on special occasions, as can be seen from the Egyptian name for the outer court, 'the court of the multitude'. Designated areas for 'making supplication and the hearing of petitions' were sometimes located within temple courts as well as on the temple's perimeters. The populace was also able to meet priests on personal matters or temple business and to deliver offerings in the open courts of many temples.

This court is usually an open court with portico-type columns on the perimeter of the court. In these courts, there are usually statues. This is reminiscent of the "statue room" in the U.S. Congress. The White House Colonnade is a portico where the president (officials) walks from public to private quarters. [For more information about the Egyptian festivals, read *Egyptian Mystics: Seekers of The Way* by Moustafa Gadalla.]

13.5 DEACTIVATION OF ENERGY (DEFACEMENTS)

We have seen how the Ancient Egyptian temple was designed, in whole and in part, to be a living organic building; to communicate between Earth and heavenly powers that can produce energy for the benefit of people and the land. The divine energies flowed uninterrupted—through proper rituals—throughout the temple.

The Hermetic Texts read:

> *"...in Egypt all the operations of the powers which rule and work in heaven have been transferred to earth below...it should rather be said that the whole cosmos dwells in [Egypt] as in its sanctuary..."*

The Egyptians were masters in predicting events in the future, including the demise of the Pharaonic Era. The Hermetic Texts also told us:

> *"There will come a time when ... the deities will return from earth to heaven; Egypt will be forsaken, and the land which was once the home of religion will be left desolate, bereft of the presence of its deities."*

Sensing the end of an era, the Egyptian priests used selective chiseling in monuments. The intent was to de-activate the flow of energy in the temples so that the subsequent dark forces are unable to abuse the cosmic energies.

The defacement were selective—some of the defaced areas are very difficult to reach, which would have required extensive preparation and platforms so the defacer could carefully and selectively chisel certain portions so neatly.

Here in the Edfu Temple, chiseling was so selective and was located so high up that it required special effort and many hours.

Further south, in Aswan, we find a similar situation in the Philae Temple. Noteworthy are the perfectly and neatly chiseled figures on the outer pylon of the temple.

The Ancient Egyptians buried thousands of statues, ritual tools, and vessels throughout the country to deactivate their temples. The noses on some statues were intentionally broken off, and are not the casual effect of rough handling or damage due to time. The statue was intended as a "living" representation. The statue, like the man, received *the breath of life through the nostrils* (a very common expression in Egyptian). By breaking off the nose, the statue was deprived of its "life".

The Hermetic Texts that predicted the demise of the Pharaonic Era also predicted its revival. For the text reads:

"But when all this has befallen, then the Master and Father, God, the first before all, will look on that which has come to pass, and will stay the disorder by the counter-working of his will, which is the good. He will call back to the right path those who have gone astray; he will cleanse the world from evil. . .

Such is the new birth of the cosmos; it is a making again of all things good, a holy and awe-striking restoration of all nature; and it is wrought in the process of time by the eternal will of God."

The Old Spirits will come back home.

APPENDICES

Appendix A: General Plans of Sample Egyptian Temples

Egyptian temples are found throughout Egypt proper and beyond in Sudan as well as in the Eastern and Western Deserts and the Sinai Peninsula. They were built for various purposes and, accordingly, they vary in size.

In addition to other temples discussed in the text of this book, we will show herein the general layout plans of several other Egyptian temples, including short descriptions of each.

1. Classical Pyramid Complex

The Egyptian masonry pyramids were harmonically proportioned to act/function in the same fashion as greenhouses, i.e. to attract and retain certain energies. These masonry pyramids were closed and sealed structures. They were not open for daily activities/rituals, which was the case in the Egyptian temples.

Each of the stone pyramids of the 4th Dynasty (those at Meidum, Dahshur [Bent and Red Pyramids], and at the Giza Plateau) was part of a complex that contained some temples. So, all the rituals were carried out in these temples, and not in the pyramids.

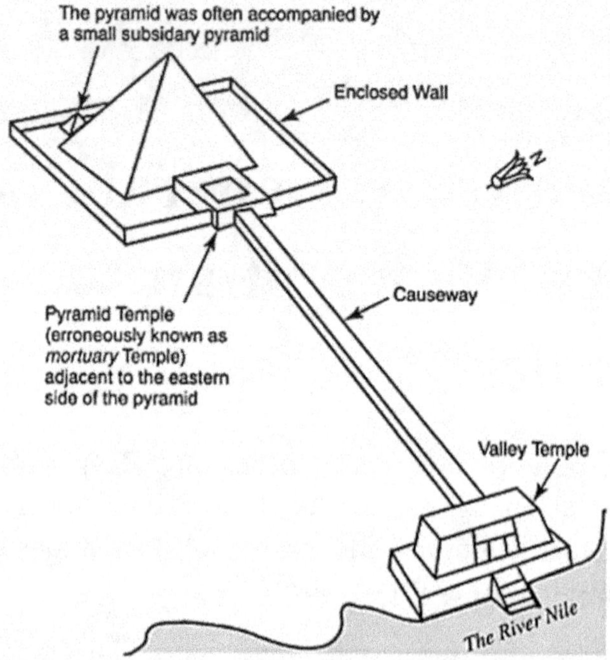

A small enclosure and a pyramid temple (erroneously known as mortuary) with a causeway to the river were constructed with all the 4th Dynasty pyramids.

For more details about these pyramids, read *Egyptian Pyramids Revisited* by Moustafa Gadalla.

2. Luxor Temple [east bank of Luxor]

Luxor Temple was called, by Ancient Egyptians, the Southern Harem (meaning 'sacred'). It is located on the eastern bank of the Nile River in the center of the city of Luxor.

The construction of this temple began in the middle Kingdom and was continuously added to until the end of the Pharaonic History of Egypt.

The main features of the temple include:

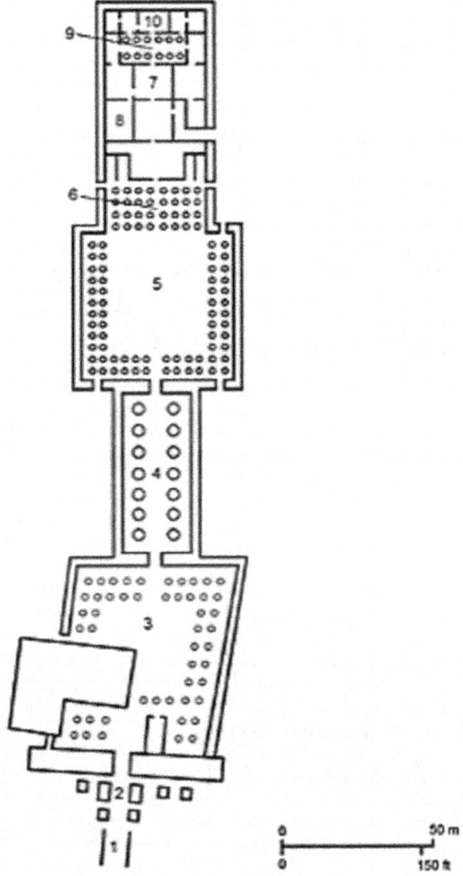

1 – The Avenue of the human-headed Sphinx originally connected this temple to the Karnak Temple, for a distance of 2 km (1.25 mi.). Only 200 m (650 feet) of these sphinxes remain, located north of the Luxor The man-headed sphinxes are exact replicas of each other.

2 – The huge pylon entrance was built by Ramses II. It also has two seated statues of the king. They were two of the original six statues, four seated and two standing. Originally, two large obelisks stood in front of the pylon. However, only one remains, while the other now stands in Place de la

Concorde, in Paris. Ramses II's symbolic battle of Kadesh is depicted on the exterior side of this pylon.

3 – The Court beyond the pylon was built by Ramses II (1304–1237 BCE), and was bordered on three sides by double rows of columns. On the northwestern side of the Court is Tuthomosis III's triple shrine. In the northeastern part of the Court is the Mosque of Abul Haggag, built on top of this Pharaonic sacred structure. Notice the striding colossus of Ramses II in the southeast corner.

4 – The Colonnade, built by Amenhotep III, has 14 smooth papyrus-shaped columns. The walls behind the columns were decorated during the reign of Tutankhamen (1361–1352 BCE), and they show the Apet Festival in great detail, with the King Tutankhamen, the nobility, and the common people joining the festival procession from the Karnak Temple.

5 – The Peristyle Court of Amenhotep III is surrounded on three sides by double rows of pillars with closed-budded capitals.

6 – The Hypostyle Hall, containing 32 pillars, connects to a room with eight columns, then to another room with four columns.

7 – The Inner Sanctuary with the Holy of Holies.

8 – The Divine (Spiritual) Marriage.

9 – Hall of the Twelve Columns is located past the Inner Sanctuary.

10 – Triple Sanctuary is at the farthest end of the Temple.

3. Temples of Karnak

The Temples of Karnak are located in Luxor, 2 km (1.25 miles) north of Luxor Temple. Its ancient name was *Apetsut,* or *The Numerator of Places.*

The original sanctuary of the Temple was built during the Middle Kingdom period. The oldest part of the complex is the White Pavillion of Sen-usert (Sesostris) I (1971-1926 BCE). The rest of the temples, pylons, courts, columns and reliefs were the work of New Kingdom Pharaohs.

The main axis (west-east) of the temple:

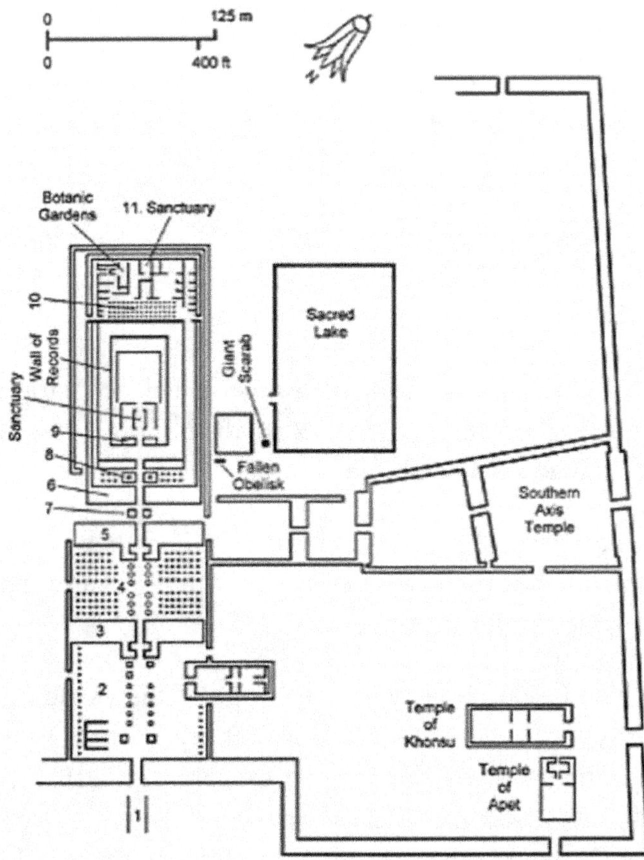

1 – The Avenue of the Rams, which is a pathway, is lined with sphinxes with heads of rams, each one exactly like the next, with great precision. It was used to link the first pylon to the east bank of the Nile.

The first and largest pylon is 113 m (370 feet) wide and 15 m (50 ft.) high.

2 – The Great Courtyard includes the following features:

– On the far right, there is the Temple of Ramses III, with its courtyard surrounded on three sides by the Osrein pillars.

– To the left is the triple shrine. The three small chapels held the sacred barques during the lead-up to the Apet Festival.

– The middle of the Court contains the remains of a double colonnade built by King Taharqa (690–664 BCE).

– A portico of strong columns with closed papyrus capitals is on the left side. Next to them is a row of ram-headed sphinxes, by Ramses II.

3 – The Second Pylon was built by Horemheb (1348–1335 BCE). Ramses II erected two colossal pink granite statues on both sides of the entrance.

4 – The Great Hypostyle Hall is one of the world's greatest architectural masterpieces. It is 102 m x 53 m (335 ft. x 174 ft.). It began with Amenhotep (Amenophis) III, continued with Seti I, and finished by Ramses II. It has 134 columns, 24 m (79 feet) high. The columns' circumference is 10 m (33 feet), and the top of the open papyrus-shaped capital is 15 m

(50 feet). All columns and walls are fully inscripted and decorated. The outer walls of this Hall are decorated with some of the records of Seti I (1333–1304 BCE) and Ramses II.

5 – The Third Pylon was built by Amenhotep III.

6 – The Fourth Pylon was built by Tuthomosis I.

7 – A Narrow Court lies between the Third and Fourth Pylons. Tuthomosis I (1528–1510 BCE) raised two obelisks in front of the Fourth Pylon. Only one is still standing. The obelisk of Tuthomosis I, is 22 m (70 feet) high and 143 tons in weight.

8 – The Fifth Pylon was constructed by Tuthomosis I. In front of this pylon, Hatshepsut (1490–1468 BCE) raised two obelisks. Only one is standing. The Hatshepsut Obelisk is 30 m (98 ft.) in height and weighs 320 tons. Tuthomosis III built a 25 m (82 fet) high sandstone structure around Hatshepsut's obelisk. Hatshepsut's other obelisk lies broken near the Sacred Lake of the Karnak Temple.

9 – The Sixth Pylon, now in a ruined state, was built by Tuthomosis III. It leads to the sacred barque sanctuary, and long lists of Tuthomosis III's records are depicted on surrounding walls. The sanctuary was first constructed during the Middle Kingdom.

10 – The Hall of Ceremonies (Akh-Menu) is located past the central court, dates back to the Middle Kingdom and leads to a large Hall of Ceremonies built by Tuthomosis III.

11 – The Last Sanctuary (Holy of Holies) is located beyond the Festival Hall. One of the three rooms that form this sanctuary contains what is called "The Botanical Garden". The room walls are carved with plants and animals from different parts of the world.

<u>**Karnak's Southern Axis**</u>

The southern axis begins between the 3rd and 4th Pylons of the main west-east axis. It has a small hypostyle hall, several pylons, and a ruined sanctuary. The temple was started by Ramses III, and was added to by other Pharaohs.

Other Points of Interest at Karnak Complex:

1 – The Temple of Khonsu is in a fairly good state of repair. It has a small hypostyle hall and a ruined sanctuary. The temple was started by Ramses III and added to by other pharaohs.

2 – The Temple of Apet is dedicated to the hippopotamus-netert (goddess) Apet. A 2 km (1.25 mile)-long avenue of human-headed sphinxes connected the Temple of Apet to the Luxor Temple.

3 – The Pavilion of Senusert (Sesostris) I is the oldest structure in the Karnak Complex. Sen-usert I (1971–1926 BCE) built this very harmonious architectural gem. It contains plenty of geodesic information, such as all the provinces of Egypt with each's respective surface area, as well as the Nile normal flood elevations at three main points along the river.

4 – The Sacred Lake was used for purification ceremonies of the priests. It drew its water from the Nile. The lake was 120 m x 77 m (400 ft. x 250 feet) and was surrounded by buildings, storehouses, an aviary, and housing for the priests.

<u>**4. Hatshepsut Temple**</u>

Hatshepsut's (1490 to 1468 BCE) temple is located on the west bank of the Nile in Luxor. It is very similar to an earlier temple that was built 600 years earlier by the Mentuhoteps, the kings of the 9th Dynasty. The ruins of the earlier temple are located to the south, next to Hatshepsut's Temple.

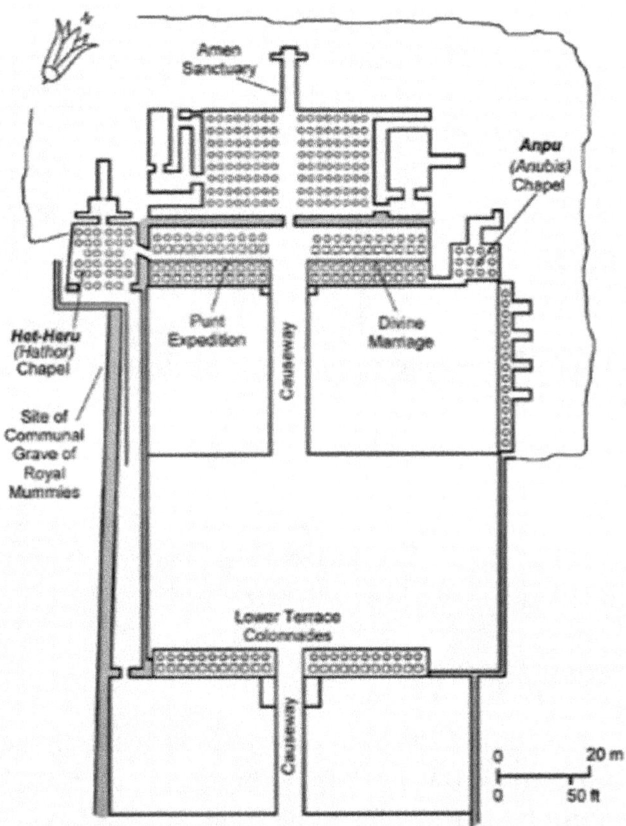

Hatshepsut's Temple consists of:

1 – A causeway, 36 m (120 feet) wide, that leads onto the three huge terraced courts.

2 – The lower terrace consists of a double colonnade formed of two rows of eleven columns on each side of the ramp. The walls around the colonnades feature scenes of bird-catching with nets, and the transport of a pair of obelisks.

3 – The central terrace contains:

– Double colonnades of 11 columns on the right side. The walls there depict the "Divine Conception" of Hatshepsut.

– Double colonnades of 11 columns on the left side. The walls there depict the naval expedition that she dispatched to the legendary land of Punt.

– On the far right, there is the Anubis Shrine, with colorful reliefs.

– On the far left is the chapel of Hathor, which contains 14 Hathor-headed columns. This leads into successive rock-hewn rooms, which lead to the shrine. The walls throughout have fine, colorful reliefs.

4 – The third terrace has now been restored. The sanctuary is located at the end of the temple. This sanctuary is hewn out of the cliff.

5. Ramesseum Temple

This temple is located on the western Nile bank of the city of Luxor. Ramses II (1304–1237 BCE) built this temple. The main features of this [now ruined] temple include:

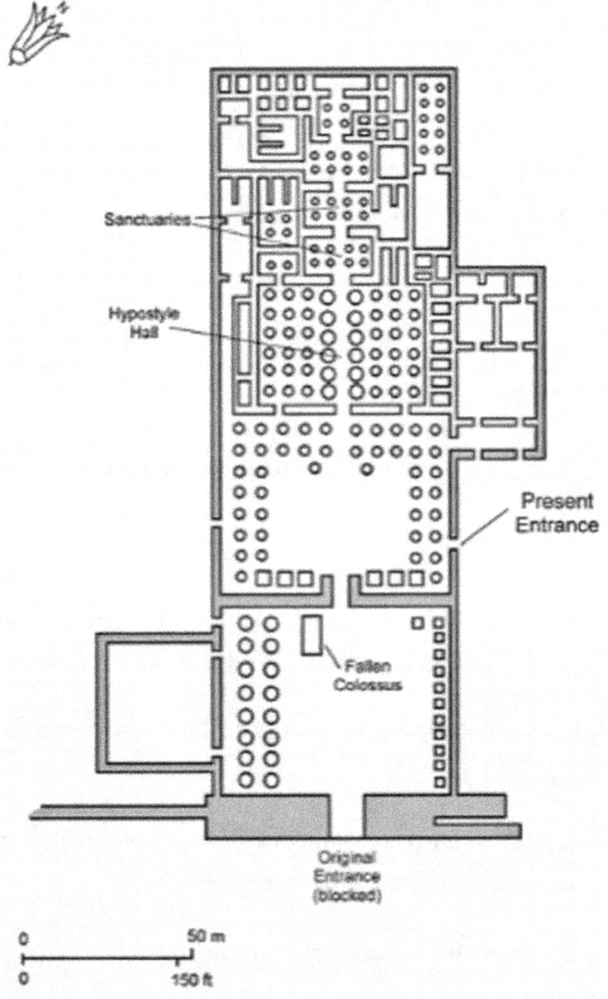

1 – The huge 1st and 2nd pylons, which feature reliefs of Ramses' symbolic battle of Kadesh.

2 – The Great Court includes the double colonnades (in a ruined state). Near the western stairs is part of the Colossus of Ramses II. When it stood, it was 18 m (60 feet); with his crown, it was 23 m (75 feet) high. It is said that the Persian King Cambyses destroyed it, in about 526 BCE. Others say that it was the result of an earthquake in 27 BCE.

3 – The Great Hypostyle Hall has 29 of the original 48 columns still standing. The ceiling here features astronomical scenes and provides information on the Egyptian calendrical system. The hall contains three naves, in which the outer columns are fitted with closed bud capitals and the inner with opened bud capitals.

4 – Sanctuaries and surrounding rooms are now in a ruined state.

6. Medinet Habu Temples

This temple complex is located on the western Nile bank of the city of Luxor.

The work on this site was begun by Amenhotep I (1550–1528 BCE) and was added to by Hatshepsut, Tuthmosis III, and other rulers right through to the end of the Pharaonic history of Egypt.

This temple complex is second only to the Temples of Karnak in size and complexity.

The wall reliefs here are enormous. The reliefs are neatly cut, as much as 20 cm (8 in.) deep into the walls.

The main features of this complex include:

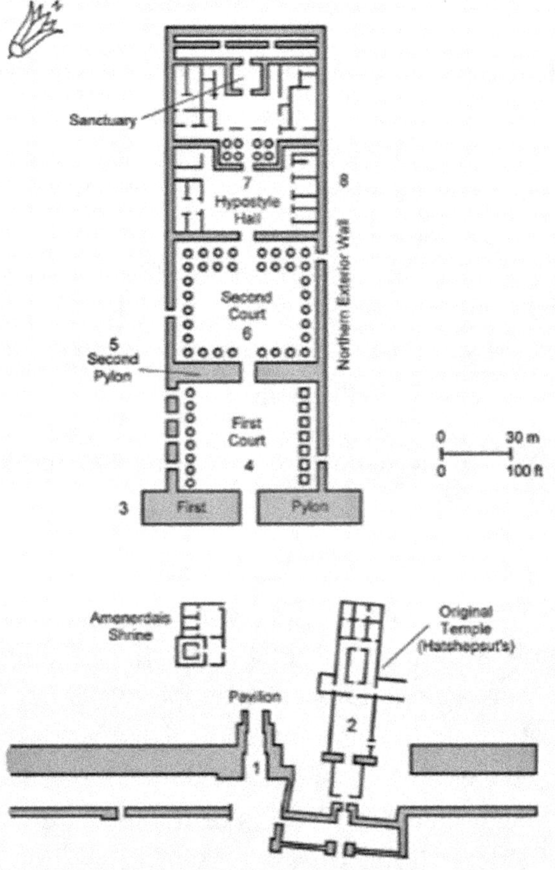

1 – The Pavilion looks like a fort, with the usual scenes of the powers of light defeating the powers of darkness.

2 – The Original Temple (known as the Temple of Hatshepsut) is a small temple was built by Amenhotep I, and completed by Hatshepsut. Many Pharaohs left their marks here: Tuthomosis III, Akhenaton, Horemheb, and Seti I.

3 – The First Pylon is covered on both sides with representations and inscriptions of symbolic depictions.

4 – The First Court contains columns with statues in the Osiris form.

5 – The Second Pylon shows other inscriptions.

6 – The Second Court has very interesting wall reliefs behind the colonnades. The walls depict Festivals of Min and Ptah-Sakar-Osiris. The walls also show scenes related to the creation mysteries.

7 – The Third Court, Offices, and Sanctuaries. This area was originally roofed over. The walls include beautiful reliefs of various objects: musical instruments, jewelry, and other arti-facts.

8 – The Northern Exterior Wall depicts the naval battle against the "Peoples of the Sea".

The "Peoples of the Sea" began their mass invasion of the coastal plain of Canaan (present-day Israel, Palestine, and Lebanon) around 1174 BCE, which coincided with the Greek war against Troy. The temple walls here depict the fact that the invading people consisted of fighters as well as refugees with their whole families. The wall inscriptions also indicate that the "Peoples of the Sea" were a combina-tion of Peleset (Philistines—the word Palestine came from Peleset), Tjekker, Sheklesh, Danu and Weshesh. Ramses III defeated the invaders in a naval battle, but allowed the fam-ily refugees to settle in southwest Canaan.

7. Dendara Temple

Dendera (Enet-ta-ntr) is located about 50 km (30 miles) north of Luxor. Enet-ta-ntr is the Ancient Egyptian name for Dendera. Dendera's main Temple of Het-Hathor was called "Pr Het-Heru" meaning "House of Het-Heru". It was a major healing centre for people from all over.

The inscription on the present temple states that the original building was erected in the far pre-Dynastic times by "the followers of Horus". Archaeological evidence shows that Khufu (the builder of the Great Pyramid) built a temple, presumably on this temple site. During the reign of Pepi I (2289–2255 BCE), the Enet-ta-ntr Temple was rebuilt. Several subsequent Pharaohs left their marks in this important site.

As with such ancient temples, they require restoration every few decades/centuries. This temple was last restored by the Egyptians during the Greco-Roman period.

The Dendera (Enet-ta-ntr) site's main features:

1 – Hathor Main Temple

The main features of this beautiful temple include:

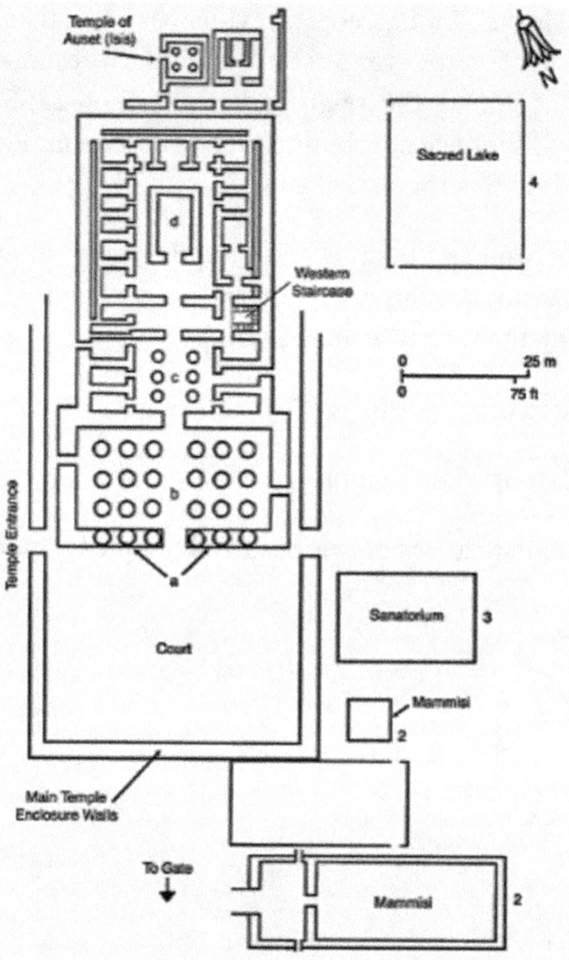

a. The temple facade contains six Hathor-headed sistrum columns and a huge corniche.

b. The Great Hypostyle Hall has 18 similar Hathor-headed columns. The ceiling has a very interesting astronomical decoration with a representation of the twelve signs of the zodiac.

c. The Small Hypostyle Hall contains six Hathor-headed columns. This and several surrounding rooms are fully decorated with interesting scenes.

d. The Decorated Sanctuary and surrounding rooms.

e. The Roof Chapels and Sanctuaries are fully decorated. A part of its ceiling is carved with the famous circular Dendera zodiac. (Actually, the present zodiac is a plaster cast of the original, which is now in the Louvre.)

2 – Mammisi (The Birth Houses)

There are two Mammisi from two different periods. The reliefs on the walls of both birth houses depict the "Divine Birth" (similar to Luxor and Hatshepsut Temples).

3 – Sanatorium

4 – Sacred Lake

8. Abydos Temples

This is one of Egypt's most complete temples. The relief carving during Seti's reign (1306–1290 BCE) is the best of the New Kingdom. Every centimeter of the temple walls are covered with perfectly executed scenes. The Seti Temple was begun by Seti I, and was completed in lesser quality during the reign of his successor, Ramses II.

Points of main interest:

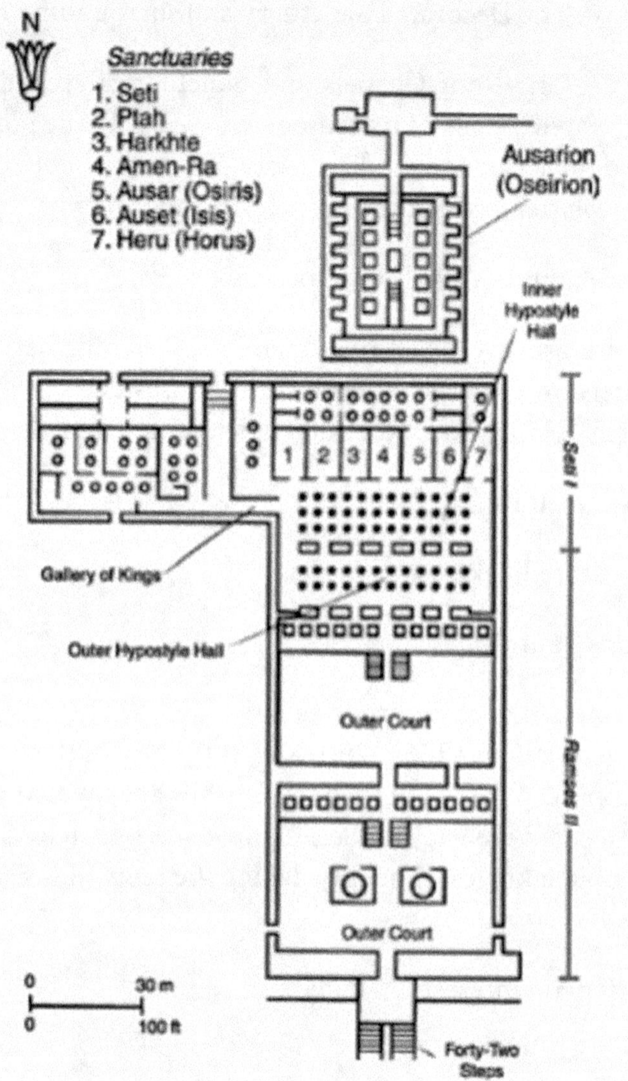

1 – The Temple begins at the top of 42 steps, representing the 42 assessors of the Duat where Osiris presides in the final judgment day.

2 – The temple is L-shaped and has seven sanctuaries.

3 – The Osiris Chapel has an overview of the various forms

and functions of Osiris as symbolized by different head-dresses, emblems and gestures.

The Oseirion

The Oseirion consists of huge red granite pillars, each weighing about 100 tons. The outer walls are built of red sandstone.

The Oseirion building is very similar to the Valley Temple of Khafra (Chephren), south of the Sphinx at Giza. Both have the same massive simplicity, the mighty square granite pillars and the total absence of inscriptions and carvings.

The Oseirion structure is partially submerged underneath the present groundwater table. The present level of the water table has risen some 6 m (20 feet) since New Kingdom times.

Because Seti I inscribed his name on some parts of the building, some academians were quick to attribute the building of the Oseirion to Seti I. It was, however, a common practice for pharaohs to inscribe their names on others' temples and monuments.

The Oseirion is extremely different from any other building in the New Kingdom. There is a huge difference between its massive, bare, and brutal simplicity as compared to the elegant and sophisticated main temple of Seti I. The Oseirion constitutes an extreme contrast in architecture, style and design to Seti's temple.

The tremendous difference in elevation between the Oseirion and Seti's Temple, as well as the dramatic difference in style between the two, suggested to many scholars that the Oseirion is a much older building. The evidence at the Oseirion and other funerary remains at Abydos is consistent with the evidence at Giza and elsewhere, regarding the antiquity of the Egyptian civilization, which is much older than academicians are willing to admit.

Osiris Temple of Ramses II

Ramses II built another temple dedicated to Osiris, just northwest of Seti I's temple. The roof of this temple has collapsed, but the walls still stand, displaying interesting reliefs.

9. Esna Temple

Esna's Temple is located 50 km (30 miles) south of Luxor. It is dedicated to Khnum, an Egyptian name that means "moulder". He is usually shown as a ram-headed deity, fashioning people out of clay at his potter's wheel.

The last time this temple was restored was during the time of Ptolemy VI Philometer, on the remains of a preceding 18th Dynasty sanctuary that was itself built over the ruins of earlier temples. The temple is situated about 9 m (30 feet) below the modern street level.

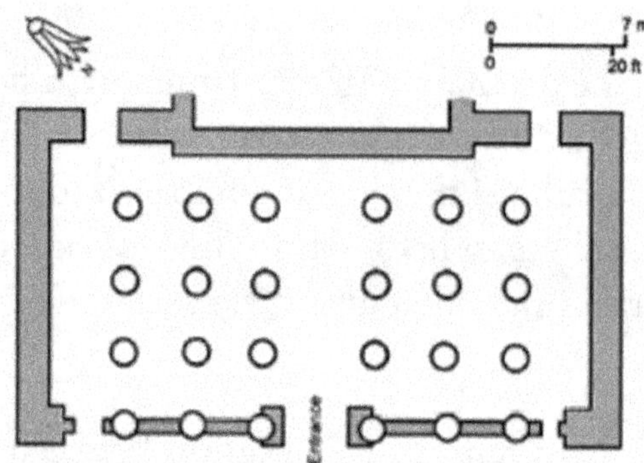

Originally, it must have been a typical full-fledged Egyptian temple. Everything vanished except the hypostyle hall—a forest of 24 columns. The columns are 13 m (43 feet) high, each fully decorated. Each column has a different capital that imitates the shapes of flowers and plants. The ceiling has a very interesting rendering of the zodiac and astronomical scenes. The interior and exterior walls are also fully decorated.

10. Edfu Temple

Edfu Temple is located 90 km (55 miles) south of Esna and 110 km (70 miles) north of Aswan. The temple plan is extremely homogeneous and, as such, it qualifies as the archetype of the Egyptian temple.

The main features of this temple include:

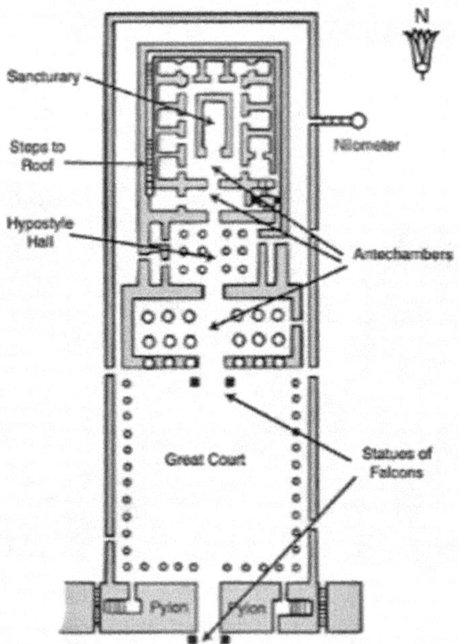

1 – The entrance to the temple is through a huge pylon, and is guarded by two beautiful granite falcons.

2 – The Great Court has a colonnade of 32 columns on three sides, and is covered with beautiful reliefs.

3 – An Antechamber that contains 18 columns. There are another two majestic black granite statues of the falcon Horus, wearing the symbolic double crown, at its entrance.

4 – A Hypostyle Hall contains 12 columns, fully decorated.

5 – Two fully decorated Antechambers are situated beyond the Hypostyle Hall.

6 – The Sanctuary of Horus is encircled with ten chapels.

7 – All interior and exterior walls are fully decorated with symbolic representations.

8 – The Mammisi (Birth House) is located near the temple, and depicts the usual divine (spiritual) birth.

11. Kom Ombo Temple

Kom Ombo's main attraction is its dual Temple of the crocodile-headed Sebek and the falcon-headed Heru-ur (Haroeris). It is a double purpose, symmetrical temple. The temple dates to a pre-dynastic era, and was restored every few centuries.

The main features of the site include:

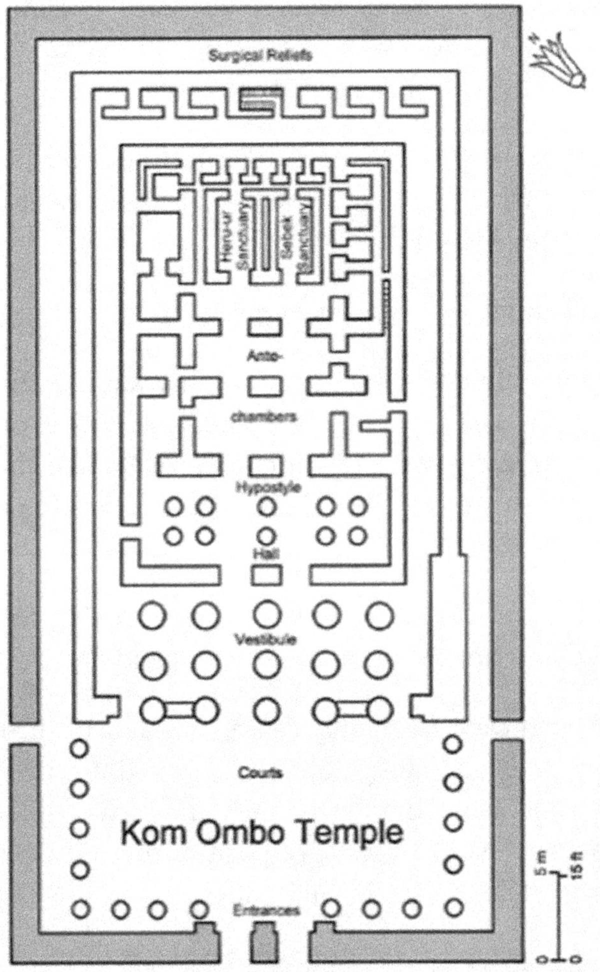

1 – There are double entrances, courts, colonnades (in a ruined state), hypostyle halls, and sanctuaries. All interior and exterior walls, as well as all the remaining columns, are fully decorated with beautiful hieroglyphs and symbolic representations.

2 – On the outer corridor wall of the temple is a box of surgical instruments, carved in relief. The box contains metal shears, surgical knives, saws, probes, spatulas, small hooks and forceps.

3 – South of the main temple is the Chapel of Hathor, which is now used to keep a large collection of mummified crocodiles that came from a nearby cemetery.

4 – The ruins of the Mammisi (Birth House) are located outside the main pylon, and served as the usual divine (spiritual) birthplace of Horus.

12. Philae Temple of Isis in Aswan

This ancient temple was built on a site that was used previously, and its Egyptian name, meaning Island of the Time of Re, suggests an extremely remote antiquity. As would have been expected, such an ancient temple required restoration every few centuries.

In the Osiris and Isis allegory, Isis while searching for the dismembered pieces of Osiris, found her husband's heart on Philae.

The old Aswan Dam frequently caused flooding of the temple in Philae, but the High Dam guaranteed to flood it forever. Before the High Dam was completed, the temple was relocated on nearby Agilka Island. It was re-positioned to correspond as closely as possible to its original location.

The main features of this temple complex include:

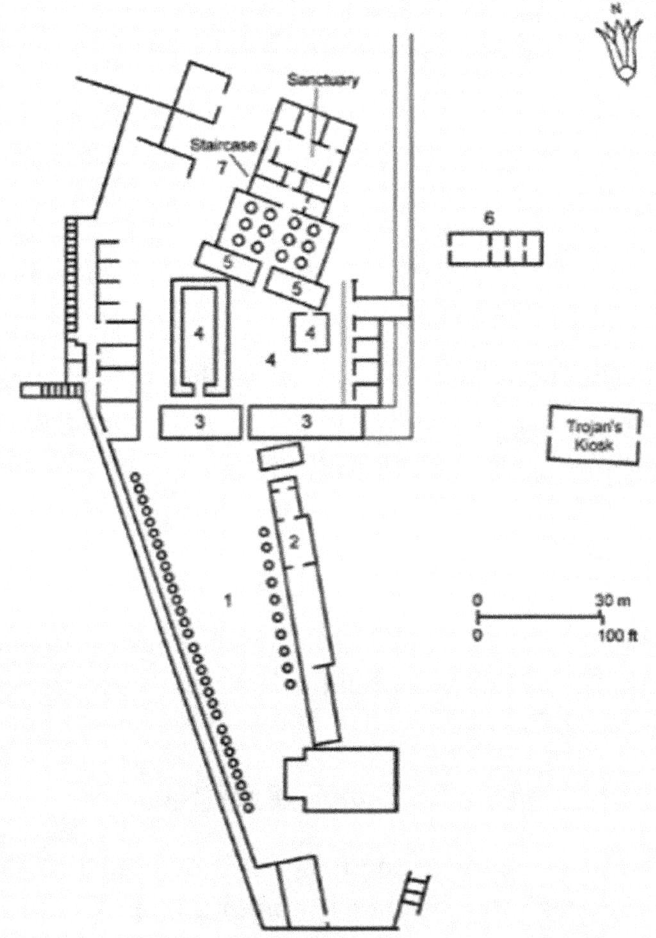

1 – The First Pylon has beautiful wall carvings.

2 – The Great Court, has 31 (originally 32) beautiful columns with various floral capitals on the west side, and six columns on the east side.

3 – A small temple, dedicated to Imhotep, is located at the rear of the eastern colonnade.

4 – The Central Court includes a Mammisi (birth-house),

dedicated to Horus. At the northeast corner of the Court is a building that was used as a healing center.

5 – The Second Pylon has intriguing depictions in its carvings. It also provides access to the Vestibule and the Inner Sanctuary.

6 – The Temple of Hathor, east of the second pylon, is beautifully decorated.

7 – The Osiris Chambers can be reached via a staircase at the western side of the second pylon. The Chambers are fully decorated with beautiful images of Osiris, Isis, and other deities that took part in the Osiris and Isis allegory.

13. Abu Simbel Temples

Abu Simbel is located 275 km (170 mi.) south of Aswan. It has two temples, which were built 3,200 years ago by Ramses II (1304–1237 BCE).

The Greater Abu Simbel Temple (Ramses II)

The first, and largest of the temples, is dedicated to the neter (god) Re-Harakhuti. The main features include:

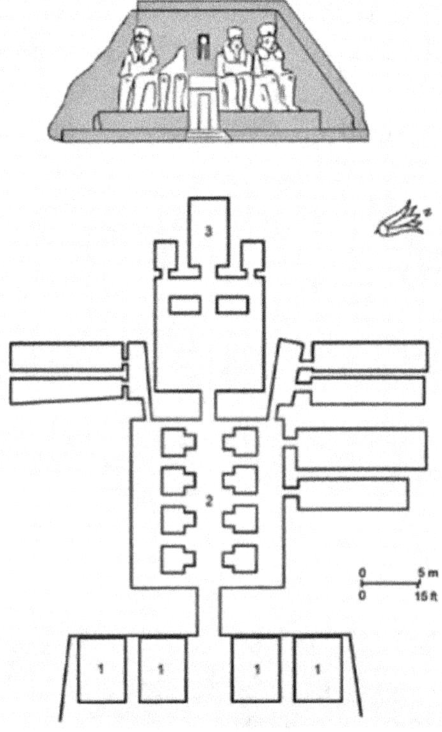

1 – The facade is 33 m (110 ft.) high, and 38 m (125 ft.) broad, and guarded by four huge seated statues, each of which is 20 m (66 ft.) high.

2 – The Great Hall of Pillars is located beyond the entrance. It has eight Osiris pillars. The wall and column reliefs here depict the typical symbolic victorious king, against his enemies. Other side rooms are fully decorated with ceremonial representations.

3 – The Holiest of Holies is 55 m (180 ft.) back into the living rock, where there are four sitting statues. The sun shines directly on the Holiest of Holiest two days a year: February 22. After the relocation of the temple, the dates are now February 23 and October 23.

The Smaller Abu Simbel Temple

This temple is located a short distance from the main temple. It was carved in the rock. The facade is adorned by six statues, in the form of Hathor, netert (goddess). The interiors look like the interior of the main temple.

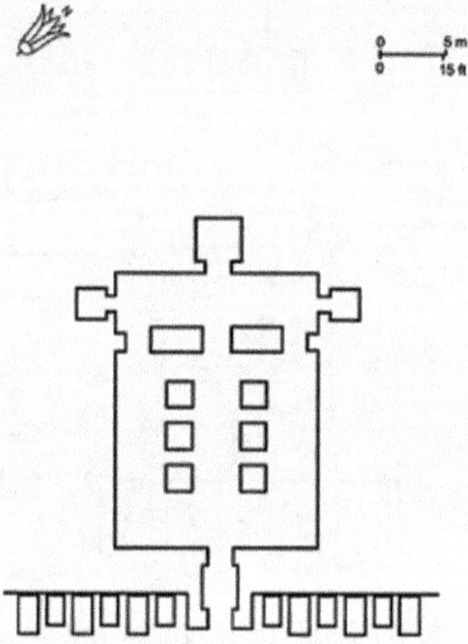

The Relocation of Abu Simbel Temples

These two temples attracted worldwide attention when they were threatened by inundation by the rising waters of the High Dam. In response to an appeal by Egypt in 1959, UNESCO initiated an international donations campaign to save these monuments. The rescue of the Abu Simbel temples began in 1963. To save it from inundation, the temples, weighing about 40,000 tons, were cut into 2,000 pieces, moved 28 m (90 ft.) higher, and reassembled on a higher plateau.

Appendix B: Practical Mathematics in Ancient Egypt

The numerous monuments of Ancient Egypt, with their perfect construction, attest to their superior knowledge (among other things) of mathematics and geometry.

The Ancient Egyptians never formulated or worked out problems for frivolous purposes just to show off their capabilities. To do so would be an exercise in vanity and useless number gymnastics.

The Egyptians had a system of decimal numbering, with a sign for 1, another for 10, 100, 1000 and so on. The evidence at the beginning of the 1st Dynasty (2575 BCE) shows that the system of notation was known up to the sign for 1,000,000.

All that is known of Egyptian "mathematics" comes from a Middle Kingdom papyrus and a few fragments of other texts of a similar nature. The study of mathematics began long before the "mathematical" papyri were written. These found papyri are not a mathematical treatise in the modern sense – that is to say, they do not contain a series of rules for dealing with problems of different kinds – but are merely a series of tables and examples worked out with the aid of the tables.

The four most referred to papyri are:

1. The Rhind "Mathematical" Papyrus (now in the British

Museum) is a copy of an older document during King Nemara (1849–1801 BCE), 12th Dynasty. It contains a number of examples to which academic Egyptologists have given the serial numbers 1-84.

The heading of this Ancient Egyptian Papyrus reads:

> **'*Rules for enquiring into nature and for knowing all that exists, every mystery, every secret.*'**

The intent is very clear that Ancient Egyptians believed and set the rules for numbers and their interactions (so-called mathematics) as the basis for "all that exists". [For more about number mysticism, read *Egyptian Cosmology* by Moustafa Gadalla.]

2. The Moscow "Mathematical" Papyrus (in the Museum of Fine Arts of Moscow) also dates from the 12th Dynasty. It contains a number of examples to which academic Egyptologists have given the serial numbers 1-19. Four examples are geometrical ones.

3. The Kahun fragments.

4. The Berlin Papyrus 6619, which consists of four fragments reproduced under the numbers 1-4.

Below is a synopsis of the contents of the Rhind "Mathematical" Papyrus:

- Arithmetic

  - Division of various numbers.
  - Multiplication of fractions.
  - Solutions of equations of the first degree.
  - Division of items in unequal proportions.

- Measurement

– Volumes and cubic content of:

> cylindrical containers
> rectangular parallelopipectal

• Areas of:

> – squaring the circle
> – rectangle
> – circle
> – triangle
> – truncated triangle
> – trapezoid

• Batter or angle of a slope of a pyramid and of a cone.

• Miscellaneous problems:

> – Divisions into shares in arithmetical progression.
> – Geometrical progression.

Other Mathematical Processes known from other Papyri include:

• Square and square root of quantities involving simple fractions [Berlin 6619].

• Solution of equations of the second degree [Berlin Papyrus 6619].

• • •

It must be noted that the Rhind Papyrus shows that the calculation of the slope of the pyramid [Rhind Nos. 56-60] employs the principles of a quadrangle triangle, which is called the *Pythagoras Theorem*.

This Egyptian Papyrus is dated thousands of years before

Pythagoras walked this earth. The so-called Pythagorean Theorem should be called the Horus "Theorem", because Horus symbolizes the hypotenuse in the Ancient Egyptian traditions of the 3:4:5 triangle.

The theorem states that the square of the hypotenuse of a right triangle is equal to the sum of the squares of the other two sides. The 3:4:5 triangle represents this rule by using integer numbers for all three sides.

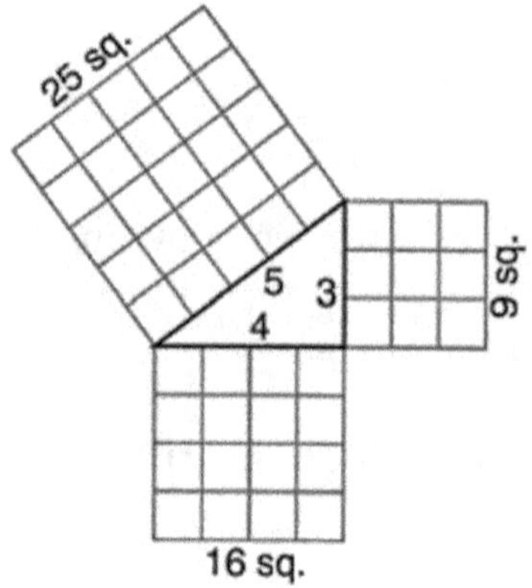

The square of side 3 = 9 squares.

The square of side 4 = 16 squares.

The square of side 5 = 25 squares.

The total of both squares (3 and 4) = 9 + 16 = 25 squares, which is the square for the hypotenuse side. The 3:4:5 triangle is as ancient as Egypt is.

•   •   •

We should not judge the level reached by the Egyptians in mathematics, because our only knowledge in this field is based on two incomplete papyri and a few fragments, almost all of which date from the Middle Kingdom. Moreover, we should not cavalierly ignore the objective of the papyri as stated at its beginning, which is the mystical aspects of numbers, fractions, and calculations.

Appendix C: Fraction Mysticism

All Egyptian thought, science, and other disciplines devolve from the concept of the mystical Primordial Scission. This starting point of creation is mentioned in every subject and practically every document. It is not idle talk – they were always focused on the beginning point, for one does not know where one is going to, if one does not know where one comes from.

In Ancient Egypt, the words of Re, revealed through Thoth, became the parts (fractions) of the world.

To Egypt, a fraction—any fraction—could only be a fraction of unity. Esoterically, because all numbers are to be regarded as divisions of unity, the mathematical relationship a number bears to unity is a key to its nature. Ancient Egypt would state "one seventh and a seventh and a seventh", but our familiar idea of 3/7 did not exist in the mind of the Egyptian.

The Ancient Egyptians represented fractions, i.e. having a numerator of 1 by drawing the mouth of Re as the numerator and unit marks underneath for the denominator.

To write $1/7^{th}$, the Egyptian simply wrote the numeral 7, in an upside-down form, underneath the mouth of Re's symbol.

A seventh is called Re-Sefkhet = mouth of seven. The glyph might be translated as *'One emits seven'*.

Heading each Ancient Egyptian numerological (so-called mathematical) papyrus that has been found, there is a table of the division of 2 by odd numbers from 3 to 101, similar to our tables of logarithms and square roots in which all fractions with a numerator of 2 are broken down into constituent fractions with a numerator of 1, which reduces the time spent for calculation. So, in practice, the Egyptian system was no more laborious than ours, and may have been less so.

Appendix D: Intentional "Irregularities" In Egyptian Works

Although the Ancient Egyptians were usually meticulous, they have always intentionally left out something (which may appear as an error) in graphic design, sculpture, painting, texts, and buildings.

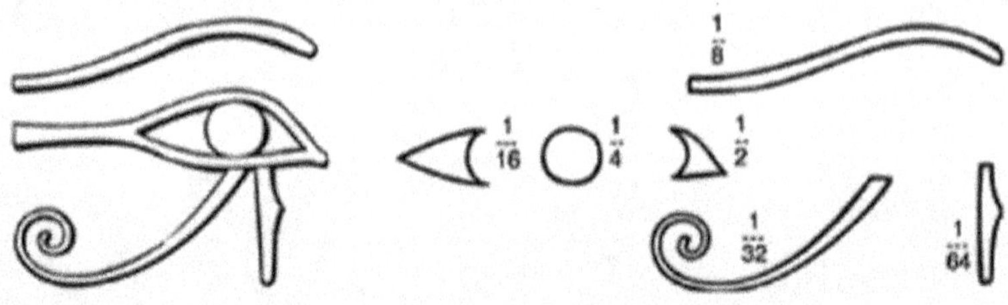

In Egypt, the sections of the eye are the glyphs for the fractions $^1/_2$ to $^1/_{64}$. The parts total $^{63}/_{64}$. The sum of successive division will always fall short of unity except at infinity, which is perfectly consonant with Egyptian thought: *only the Absolute is One*.

Appendix E: Monument Appropriations!!!

Egyptian Pharaohs are wrongly accused of "monument appropriation". The Karnak Temple is an interesting site for the study of this phenomenon. From the Middle Kingdom on, almost every king left some mark of his presence at the Karnak Temples. In some cases, a later king had removed the name of the earlier king responsible for the original building, and chiseled in his own. Some conclude, then, that the later king willfully "appropriated" the work of the earlier.

Yet, the matter is not that simple, and is more interesting than that. These appropriations are selective and not arbitrary. Only certain names in certain places have been removed. This can only be deliberate, even though the reasons and basis for such selectivity may not be fully understood.

Since the Ancient Egyptian temples are thousands of years old, a restoration/rebuilding (of each) was required every few decades/centuries. One can find temples which were torn down over and over again. Other temples were never torn down, but were carefully cared for, repaired, and periodically added to.

There is the typical standard explanation that they did it for economic or for egotistical reasons. Such simplistic answers ignore the fact that the powerful Pharaohs of the New Kingdom were in total command of unlimited riches. They did not need to save a few pennies, and they never lacked the authority to destroy others' work, if that was their intention. Most importantly, these simplistic answers don't account for the major question regarding the still-unknown, specified rules for the selectivity of appropriation.

The famed Egyptologist Schwaller de Lubicz was able, in his research, to show that there was a rational system in the dismantling and rebuilding processes. Certain blocks from an old temple were placed beneath the columns of a new temple, as if it was the seed to nourish a new plant. The Egyptian temple had its natural, organic lifetime, and when the temple had completed its predestined cycle, it was torn down, revised, or added to. Many other academicians have accepted that the re-deployment of blocks was deliberate, and that the purpose of this re-deployment was to regenerate the new temple.

Thus, when a king dismantled the work of a predecessor, that action was completely legitimized and had its own sacred meaning. Every king would understand that if he was acting out of egotism, his own works would suffer the same mistreatment after his death.

The works of the "Great Criminal Akhenaton" were razed to the ground. His case does not apply to monument appropriation. Read all background information about Akhenaton in *Historical Deception: The Untold story of Ancient Egypt* by Moustafa Gadalla.

We shall now review three interesting cases of so-called "monument appropriation."

1. The Case of Ramses II

Ramses II, the greatest builder of all Egypt, was also the greatest "appropriator." The "appropriations" of Ramses pose many questions. Sometimes Ramses cut the names of his predecessors out and inserted his own, but in other instances he did not. Sometimes he completed work begun by a previous king and gave that king appropriate credit. In many instances, when he did "appropriate" a temple, he also left many of the prior cartouches untouched and plainly visible. Yet, in other cases, he altered all the cartouches. Ramses II reigned for 67 years. He was the greatest builder in Egypt's history, since the pyramid age. No subsequent kings appropriated or reappropriated any projects of Ramses II.

2. Twthomosis I Obelisk

One of two obelisks at the Karnak Temple was erected by Twthomosis (Tuthomosis) I. No one touched this obelisk for four hundred years, though the kings during those four centuries did a lot of "usurping" and dismantling. After all this time, two kings left the original inscription in place and merely added their own on either side of the obelisk. They were Ramses IV and Ramses VI.

3. The Case of Twthomosis III and Hatshepsut

Much has been written about apparent disputes between Twthomosis III and Hatshepsut. Here are some interesting points:

A. Hatshepsut (1490–1468 BCE) built an obelisk at the Karnak Temple. This is the second tallest standing obelisk after the Egyptian made Lateran Obelisk, now standing in Rome. When Twthomosis (Tuthomosis) III came to power after Hatshepsut's death, one of his acts was to erect a high wall around Hatshepsut's obelisk that hid only its lower two-thirds and left its top third visible for miles.

The common simplistic explanation for such an action is that it was cheaper to hide the bottom two-thirds of its height than removing it. But building a wall around an obelisk leaving the top 15 ft. (4.6 m) visible for 50 miles (80 km) does not make sense. Twthomosis (Tuthomosis), the mighty king, could certainly have pulled down an obelisk in the blink of an eye if he wanted to. There has to be a better explanation for this wall. It is possible that this action was a part of the same campaign to undo some of the queen's works in a selective way, because of the matter of illegitimacy of her reign.

B. In certain instances, the queen's name has been left intact in full view of one and all. In other instances, it has been erased from hidden inaccessible shrines. It is the selectivity of the damage that has baffled and fascinated the scholars for centuries.

C. At Deir el-Bahari, two images of Hatshepsut are left intact. Also in the Hathor sanctuary, one can see Hatshepsut and Twthomosis III kneeling. She is holding an offering of milk and he is holding one of wine. There is no defacement here.

D. At Deir el-Bahari also, there is a figure of Hatshepsut's great architect, Senmut, who some theorized had an affair with Hatshepsut. Both figures of Hatshepsut and Senmut are left intact!

Appendix F: Sample Egyptian Sculpture Works

From the tomb of a sculptor (12th Dynasty):

"I was an artist skilled in my art, preeminent in my learning...I knew [how to represent] the movements of the image of a man and the carriage of a woman...the poising of the arm to bring the hippopotamus low and the movements of the runner..."

The Ancient Egyptian sculptors achieved perfection in their work, and the shapes wrought were the complex, subtle forms of the human anatomy. The huge sculptures could only have been brought to life through the sensitive hand and watchful eye of a master sculptor and with a great deal of loving care. This is the work of passion, not the work of a *slave*.

The mastery of Egyptian sculpture is evident in thousands of statues of all sizes, forms, and materials.

Here are a few examples of their work:

The Sphinx

As an artistic synthesis, the Sphinx is a work of mastery without parallel anywhere on Earth. So perfect is the fusion of lion and human that it seems organic.

One cannot help but admire this marvelous statue and the nice proportion of its head. The mastery of the sculptor is evident in his ability to preserve the exact proportion and balance of every part (nose, eyes, ears, etc.) in a face of such colossal size.

But when was the Sphinx built? And who built it? Many believe the answers are somewhere between 2520–2494 BCE, during the reign of Khafre (Chephren). But these commonly held beliefs are wrong. [For more information about the Great Sphinx of Giza, its age, and the very remote antiquity of Ancient Egypt, read *Ancient Egyptian Culture Revealed* by Moustafa Gadalla.]

The Statue of Khafra (Chephren)

This statue is generally acknowledged as one of the great masterpieces of world sculpture. In terms of technique and expressiveness, it would be a wondrous sculpture even if it were carved from some easily managed stone. But it is carved from diorite, the hardest known granite. It is housed at the Cairo Museum.

The Cross-Legged Seated Scribe Statue

One of these statues, with its lifelike eyes gazing into eternity, is housed in the Cairo Museum. The inlaid eyes of the statue have excited the admiration of many, including scholars, sculptors, and physicians.

When photographs are taken of this and other similar statues, the eyes actually look real. The Egyptologist Mariette recorded that when his workmen dug up the famous Seated Scribe, now in the

Louvre, the eyes frightened them; they thought the statue was actually alive.

The Fallen Colossus at Ramesseeum Temple—Western Luxor

The fallen colossus lies broken in several gigantic pieces. It was originally carved out of a single block of granite weighing 1,000 tons (907 metric tons). The seated colossus was originally 60 feet (18 m) high, which was the largest statue in Egypt. The Sphinx is much bigger, but it was carved, in-situ, out of the living rock.

The colossus was brought down, possibly as a result of the earthquake that shook Egypt in 27 BCE. Even in pieces on the ground, the colossus is still an awesome scene. The ear is 3½ feet (1.2 m) long, the circumference of the arm at the elbow is 17½ feet (5.3 m), the index finger is 3¼ feet (1 m) long. The workmanship is superb.

The Colossi Of Memnon

The two seated Colossi stand over 60 feet (18 m) high on the western bank of Luxor (Thebes), and originally both had crowns, so were even taller.

They are made of a pebbly, quartzose sandstone. The sandstone is extremely difficult to work and at the same time is highly porous and subject to relatively quick decay.

Appendix G: Concrete Blocks Various Types

For the reader to be informed about the differences between natural and man-made stone blocks, it is advisable to read the extensive work on this subject in the publication *Egyptian Pyramids Revisited* or its older edition, *Pyramid Handbook,* both by Moustafa Gadalla. We will highlight here just two points from this work:

1. Natural stone consists of fossil shells which lie horizontally or flat in the bedrock as a result of forming sedimentary layers of bedrock over millions of years.

The blocks of the masonry pyramids of Egypt show jumbled shells which are indicative of man-made cast stone. In any concrete, the aggregate are jumbled, and as a result, cast concrete is devoid of sedimentary layers. These pyramids consisted essentially of fossil shell limestone, a heterogeneous material very difficult to cut precisely.

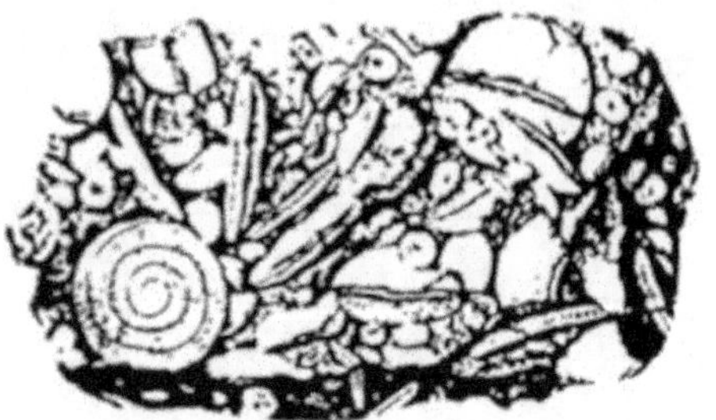

Drawing from *Description de l'Egypte,* written between 1809 and 1813 by Francois Jomard, shows jumbled shells in pyramid core blocks.

2. The French scientists found that the bulk density of the pyramid blocks is 20% lighter than the local bedrock limestone. Cast blocks are always 20-25% lighter than natural rock because they are full of air bubbles.

A man-made concrete is defined as building material made of sand and gravel, bonded together with cement into a hard, compact substance and used in making bridges, road surfaces, etc.

There are countless concrete mixes with varied ratios of the main ingredients: aggregate, cement, water and admixtures. Various applications require different concrete mixes. The Ancient Egyptians had utilized a wide variety of concrete mix applications. Examples:

In the Giza Plateau, we can find three types of concrete. At the Khufu Pyramid, for example, there are three types in the interior pyramid blocks, the exterior angled blocks, as well as the paving blocks around the pyramid site.

The interior pyramid blocks were not intended to be exposed to natural elements, therefore they were not finely graded. In other words, they were the bulk-type variety. When the exterior blocks were stripped away, these interior blocks were exposed to the natural elements. Over the years, they have deteriorated rapidly.

The exterior blocks were intended to withstand the natural elements and therefore were made of more finely graded stones, as we can see here in this photograph at the Khafra Pyramid in Giza.

Mastabas throughout the Giza Plateau utilized this strong exterior-type concrete mix in their walls, as shown herein next to Khufu Great Pyramid.

The third type of concrete mix that we can find at the Giza site is the paving blocks that surround the base of the pyramid. The exposed paving blocks at the Great Pyramid site shows us a finely graded concrete of such quality that it can withstand the abrasion forces caused by traffic.

At the Khafra Pyramid site, the paving blocks are in much better shape. They have maintained their superior qualities for thousands of years.

A fourth type of concrete block was used as harbor water breaks in Alexandria's outer harbor wall. It predates Alexander, as stated in Greek and Roman classical writings. These were designed to withstand the continuous water pressure forces of waves as well as the effect of salt in the water.

One of the seven wonders of antiquity, the Pharos (lighthouse), 140 metres high, stood on the island with the same name, in front of the harbor, and showed the way to the ships that carried valuable goods from all over the world.

Another application of concrete mixes is the type used by the Egyptians to build their arches and vaulted ceilings. Vaulted ceilings are found since the Old Kingdom in Menkaura Pyramid (in Giza) and Mastabat Faroon (in Saqqara).This and other examples were discussed earlier in Chapter 6 of this book.

Appendix H: The Masonic Egyptian Roots

The masons claim that their rites, knowledge, and traditions are rooted in Egypt, and there are many indications that this may be so.

The masons are members of a widespread secret fraternal society called 'Free and Accepted Masons' (popularly known as Freemasonry). There is a natural, instinctive fellowship and sympathy between their members.

Modern masons claim their deep roots from the Ancient Egyptians. It is interesting that the obelisk and the pyramid were important symbolic forms for them, long before Egyptology and archaeology began. The Founding Fathers of America (many of whom were masons) put the un-American pyramid on the dollar bill and chose the shape of an obelisk for the design of a monument for George Washington, who was also a mason.

Napoleon, like so many eminent men of his era, was also a Freemason. His campaign to conquer Egypt was part of his imperial military plan, but it was coupled with an intense desire to unlock the secrets of Egypt, which Napoleon believed to be the source of Masonic knowledge. Accordingly, in 1798, along with his 25,000 soldiers, he brought several hundred of the leading experts of his day, including the best draftsmen and artists in France.

One of these famed masons is Mozart. In Mozart's Masonic Opera *The Magic Flute*, the free spirit Papageno is trapping wild birds. This is purely Egyptian symbolism, because for the Ancient Egyptians, each bird (such as the falcon, vulture, stork, phoenix, goose, etc.) symbolized various spiritual qualities. Each species of bird represented a wild spiritual aspect that must be trapped, caged, sometimes tamed, and other times offered to the neteru in sacrifice.

Many other Masonic traditions are easily [and only] explained in Ancient Egyptian terms.

Appendix I: Egyptian Influence on Modern Architecture

The Egyptian influence on modern architecture is quite extensive. Several examples were specifically mentioned earlier in the text of this book. Here are a few broad, additional examples:

1 – What is described as "Spanish Architecture' or "Moorish Architecture" or "Southwestern USA" or even "Arabic/ Islamic Architecture" are all found in Ancient Egyptian construction and practices. All elements of such design are listed and described throughout the text of this book.

The design is characterized with its elegant simplicity of successive recessions and projections which is found in Egypt thousands of years earlier in the Saqqara's Zoser Complex.

The same type of design was used in the exterior of hundreds of tombs in Ancient Egypt.

Each tomb in Egypt had what is called a "false door", which was always built with successive recesses and projections.

We find the same design patterns in the most admired Hatshepsut Temple in Luxor.

2 – Throughout the major cities of the world, we always find an Egyptian Obelisk or an imitation of its form, such as the *Washington Monument* in Washington DC, the capital city of the USA.

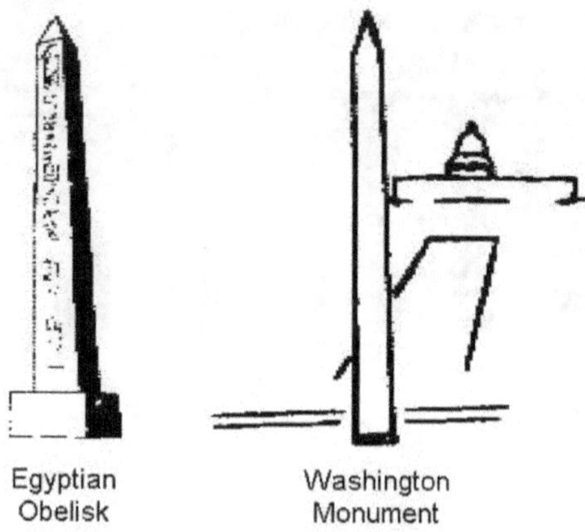

3 – Staying in the US capital city, we observe other Ancient Egyptian architectural features such as:

– The famous Oval Office of the sitting President. The oval shape resembles the outline of an Ancient Egyptian cartouche which identified the role(s)/title(s) of the Egyptian Pharaoh.

– The White House's Portico with the appearance of the sitting President is exactly like the Great Court of an Egyptian Temple.

– The US Congress roof is shaped in the form of a dome—a roof form preserved in Ancient Egypt for the Highest individuals, who become Folk Saints.

– The famous "Statuary Hall" in the US Congress looks like and serves the same purpose as an Ancient Egyptian temple with statues of dignitaries appearing/situated between the outer columns of the Hall/Court.

4 – Tomb stones in cemeteries look exactly like ancient Egyptian stelae, which also serve the same purpose as a monument of records.

Appendix J: Types and Forms of Mortals' Buildings

In conjunction with their mortal mentality, Ancient and Baladi Egyptians—the most humble—have never used the "eternal stones" for their dwelling houses. Their present life was only the pilgrimage; they were taught to consider their abode here on Earth as merely an "inn" along the road.

Despite the repeated charges of vanity against the pharaohs, it is worth remembering that their abodes while on Earth were never made of stone, but of mud brick, the same material used by the humblest peasants.

They all believed that the impermanent body, formed of clay, called for an equally impermanent abode on this Earth. The earthly houses of the kings have long since returned to the earth from which they were raised.

Varying in form and quality, the houses were all made of sun-dried brick, and sometimes made with a mixture of straw. All used this same building material, the manufacture of which occupied thousands of workers along the whole length of the Nile.

Because of the warm climate, the Egyptians lived most of their time in the open air, and the houses were constructed to be cool throughout the summer; currents of fresh air circulating freely throughout them by the practical arrangement of passages and courts. Corridors, supported on columns, gave access to different apartments through a succession of shady avenues and areas, with one side open to the air.

It is/was also common for several small Egyptian houses to share a common courtyard. The open court located in the center of the Ancient Egyptian house was planted as a garden with palms and other trees and sometimes paved with stone, with a small tank or a fountain in its center.

Most houses had a ground-floor and one or two stories above it. In major cities, houses were as tall as five stories high.

Property consisting of a house with four stories, two granaries, and an auxiliary building.

Diodorus speaks of the tall houses in Luxor (Thebes) as being four and five stories high, and Ancient Egyptian paintings show some houses with four, including the basement story.

Some roofs were vaulted, especially in the warmer areas of southern Egypt, and were built, like the rest of the house, of crude brick.

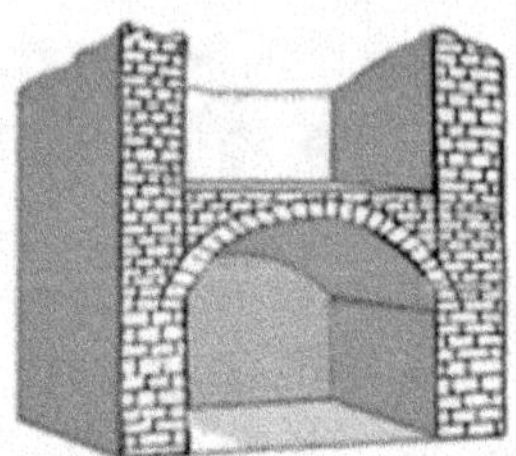

Typical Ancient Egyptian vaulted roof at Ta-Apet (Thebes).

The Ancient Egyptians utilized arches and vaulted roofs in their buildings since their earliest history. The early invention of the brick by the Ancient Egyptians led to the invention of the arch; and we find arches in Egypt as far back as the 27th century BCE, in Saqqara.

The ceilings of the Ancient Egyptian buildings were of stucco, richly painted and tasteful both in their form and the arrangement of their colors. One of the oldest decorative trims is the guilloche, often misnamed the "Tuscan" or "Greek" border.

There were also public buildings for schools, governmental offices, communal grain silos with vaulted roofs, etc.

Government bldg (partial) of the Egyptian Nome of the Gazelle.

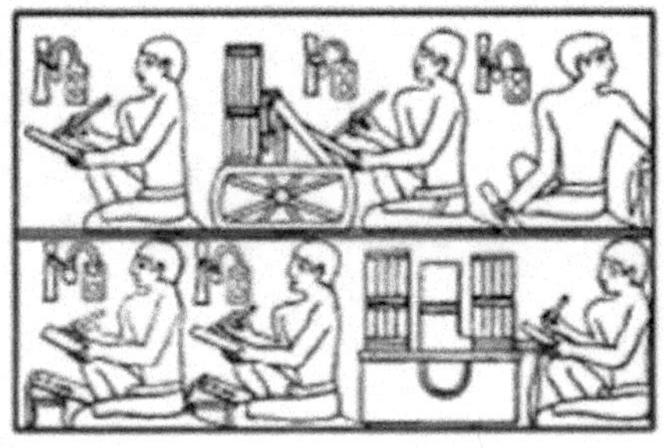

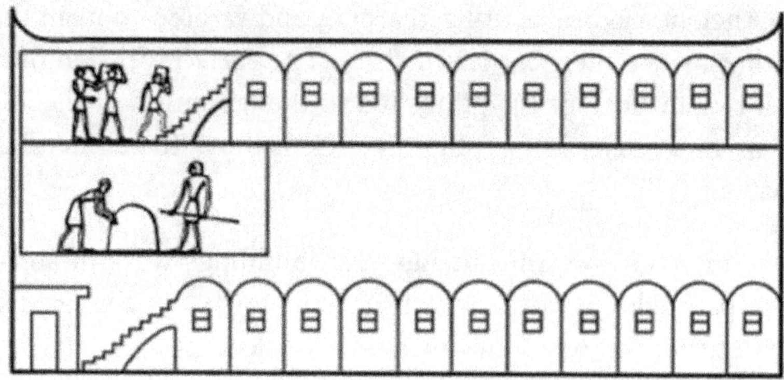

Communal grain silos, with vaulted roofs. Beni Hassan.

GLOSSARY

---

abacus – a slab that forms the uppermost member or division of the capital of a column.

amulet – a charm or ornament containing special powers or symbolic representation.

Animism – the concept that all things in the universe are animated (energized) by life forces. This concurs, scientifically, with kinetic theory, where each minute particle of any matter is in constant motion – i.e. energized with life forces.

attributes – the Divine qualities and meanings that are the real causative factors of the manifested creations.

Baladi – local; a term used to describe the present native silent majority in Egypt which adheres to the Ancient Egyptian traditions, under a thin layer of Islam.

BCE – **B**efore **C**ommon **E**ra. Also noted in other references as BC.

Book of Coming Forth By Light (Per-em-hru) – consists of over 100 chapters of varying lengths which are closely related to the so-called Pyramid Texts at Saqqara. These texts are found on papyrus scrolls that were wrapped in the mummy swathings of the deceased and buried with him.

Book of the Dead – see Book of Coming Forth By Light.

CE – Common Era. Also noted in other references as AD.

Circle Index – designates the ratio of the circumference of a circle to its diameter, and is equal to 22/7, or 3.1415927.

corolla – the inner petals of a flower.

cosmology – the study of the origin, creation, structure, and orderly operation of the universe as a whole, and of its related parts.

cubit – the Ancient Egyptian unit of linear measurement which is symbolized by the distance between the elbow and the tip of the middle finger of the extended hand. One cubit = 1.72' (0.5236 m)

Duat/Tuat – (Ancient Egypt) the Underworld, where the soul goes through transformation, leading to resurrection.

Heb-Sed – ancient festival associated with the rejuvenation of the spiritual and physical powers of the Pharaoh.

mastaba – Mastaba is the word for bench; a mud-brick, above-ground structure. Below the mastaba are the burial chambers of the deceased. The tombs consisted of subterranean burial chambers with large, low, rectangular, mud-brick superstructures.

The superstructures were rectangular, low in proportion to their lengths, and with convex roofs. They varied in size from 24 sq. yards (20 square m) to an area of more than ¼ acre.

mysticism – consists of ideas and practices that lead to union with the Divine. Union is described more accurately as togetherness, joining, arriving, conjunction, and the realization of God's uniqueness.

Neb (Golden) **Proportion** – is the "key to the structure of the cosmos". If an approximation must be made, its value is 1.6180339.

neter/netert – a divine principle/function/attribute of the One Great God. Incorrectly translated as 'god/goddess'.

ostracon – Term used by archaeologists to refer to shards of pottery or flakes of limestone bearing texts and drawings.

papyrus – could mean either: 1) A plant that is used to make a writing surface. 2) Paper, as a writing medium. 3) The text written on it, such as the Leiden Papyrus.

perfect solid – a solid figure composed of plane faces, each of whose faces is identical and is an equilateral planar form (e.g. a triangle, square or pentagon).

phi – see Neb (Golden) Proportion.

pi – see Circle Index.

polyhedron – see perfect solid.

pylon – a towering structure flanking a temple's gateway.

Pyramid Texts – a collection of transformational (funerary) literature that was found in the tombs of the 5th and 6th Dynasties (2465-2150 BCE).

sacred geometry – The process by which all figures are to be drawn or created by using only a straight line (not even a ruler) and a compass; i.e., without measurement (dependent on proportion only).

segment – A geometric shape bound by a cord and an arc of a circle.

slope (common definition) – the amount or degree of deviation from the horizontal or vertical in an inclined surface. The ratio of the vertical difference divided by the horizontal difference.

slope (in Ancient Egypt) – For the ancient Egyptians, the slope was the length required for half the base when the height was equal to 1 (one cubit).

stele (plural: stelae) – stone or wooden slab or column inscribed with commemorative texts.

vertex – the point opposite to and farthest from the base in a figure; a point that terminates a line or curve or comprises the intersection of two or more lines.

SELECTED BIBLIOGRAPHY

Aldred, Cyril. *Egyptian Art*. London, 1990.

Assmann, J. *Agyptische Hymnen Und Gebete* (*Leiden Papyrus 312-321*), Zürich/Münich, 1975.

Badawy, Alexander. *Ancient Egyptian Architectural Design*. Los Angeles, CA, USA, 1965.

Bleeker, C.J. *Egyptian Festivals: Enactments of Religious Renewal*. Leiden, 1967.

Breasted, James Henry. *Ancient Records of Egypt*, 3 Vols. Chicago, USA, 1927.

Budge, E.A. Wallis. *Amulets and Superstitions*. New York, 1978.

Budge, E.A. Wallis. *Cleopatra's Needles and Other Egyptian Obelisks*. London, 1926.

Budge, E.A. Wallis. *The Decrees of Memphis and Canopis*, 3 Vols. London, 1904.

Budge, Sir E. A. Wallis. *Egyptian Language: Easy Lessons in Egyptian Hieroglyphics*. New York, 1983.

Budge, E.A. Wallis. *Egyptian Magic*. New York, 1971.

Budge, E.A. Wallis. *Egyptian Religion: Egyptian Ideas of the Future Life.* London, 1975.

Budge, E.A. Wallis. *From Fetish to God in Ancient Egypt.* London, 1934.

Budge, E.A. Wallis. *The Gods of the Egyptians*, 2 volumes. New York, 1969.

Budge, Wallis. *Osiris & The Egyptian Resurrection* (2 volumes). New York, 1973.

Chace, Arnold Buffum. *The Rhind Mathematical Papyrus.* Ohio, USA, 1929.

Choisy, Auguste. *Historie de L'Architecture, I.* Paris, France, 1899.

DeCenival, Jean-Louis. *Living Architecture.* Tr. by K.M. Leake. New York, 1964.

Diodorus of Sicily. *Books I, II, & IV*, tr. By C.H. Oldfather. London, 1964.

Egyptian Book of the Dead (*The Book of Going Forth by Day*), The Papyrus of Ani. USA, 1991.

Erman, Adolf. *Life in Ancient Egypt.* New York, 1971.

Field, J.V. *Kepler's Geometrical Cosmology.* London, 1988.

Gadalla, Moustafa:
  – *Ancient Egyptian Culture Revealed.* USA, 2007.
  – *Egyptian Cosmology: The Animated Universe – 2nd edition.* USA, 2001.
  – *Egyptian Divinities: The All Who Are THE ONE.* USA, 2001.
  – *Egyptian Harmony: The Visual Music.* USA, 2000.
  – *Egyptian Mystics: Seekers of the Way.* USA, 2003.
  – *Historical Deception: The Untold Story of Ancient Egypt.* USA, 1999.
  – *Egypt: A Practical Guide.* USA, 1998.
  – *Pyramid Handbook.* USA, 2000.

Hambidge, Jay. *Dynamic Symmetry.* NYC, USA, 1920.

Hambidge, Jay. *Dynamic Symmetry in Composition.* Mass., USA, 1923.

Herodotus. *The Histories*. Tr. By Aubrey DeSelincourt. London, 1996.

James, T.G.H. *An Introduction to Ancient Egypt*. London, 1979.

Kastor, Joseph. *Wings of the Falcon, Life and Thought of Ancient Egypt*. USA, 1968.

Kepler, Johannes. *The Secret of the Universe*. Tr. by A.M. Duncan. New York, 1981.

Maspero,Gaston. *Manual of Egyptian Archaeology*, London, 1902

Moessel, E. *Die Proportion in Antike und Mittelalter*. München, Germany, 1926.

Peet, T. Eric. *The Rhind Mathematical Papyrus*. London, 1923.

Pennick, Nigel. *Sacred Geometry*. New York, 1982.

Piankoff, Alexandre. *The Litany of Re*. NY, NY, 1964.

Plato. *The Collected Dialogues of Plato including the Letters*. Edited by Edith Hamilton & Huntington Cairns. New York, NY, USA, 1961.

Plutarch. *Plutarch's Moralia, Volume V*. Tr. by Frank Cole Babbitt. London, 1927.

Pritchard, James B., Ed. *Ancient Near Eastern Texts*. Princeton, NJ, USA, 1955.

Siculus, *Diodorus*. Vol. 1. Tr. by C.H. Oldfather. London.

Wilkinson, J. Gardner. *The Ancient Egyptians: Their Life and Customs*. London, 1988.

Wilkinson, Richard H.
- *Temples of Ancient Egypt*, New York, 2000.
- *Reading Egyptian Art*. NY, NY, 1994.
- *Symbol & Magic in Egyptian Art*, New York, 1999.

Several Internet Sources.

Numerous references in Arabic language.

3

SOURCES AND NOTES

As a graduate civil engineer with over 40 years of experience, the author is more than qualified to comment on matters related to mathematics, geometry, building materials, and construction techniques. Academic Egyptologists are basically archaeologists whose views on technical issues are beyond their qualifications.

Almost all my sources are written by very biased authors who (consciously or sub-consciously) have pro-Western and/or Judeo-Christian paradigms. The vast majority of these references are condescending or show a disdain for Ancient Egyptians and their traditions.

Listed references in the previous section, Selected Bibliography, are only referred to for facts, events, and dates, not for their interpretations of such information.

The absence of several references in the Selected Bibliography does not mean that the author is unfamiliar with them. It only means that despite their popularity, they contain no valuable factual information.

It should be noted that if a reference is made to one of author Moustafa Gadalla's books, that each of his book contains appendices for its own extensive bibliography as well as detailed Sources and Notes.

<u>Chapter 1</u>: The Architectural Canon – Badawy, Choisy, De Cenival, Moessel, Pennick, Gadalla [Harmony, Cosmology, Divinities]

<u>Chapter 2</u>: The Metaphysical Structure of The universe – Kastor, Gadalla [Cosmology, Mystics, Divinities], Budge [Osiris], Erman

<u>Chapter 3</u>: Visitation Sites of The Lower Heavenly Court – Maspero, Erman, Wilkinson [all], James, Gadalla [Pyramid, Mystics, Cosmology, Culture, Guide], Budge [Osiris, Religion], Erman

<u>Chapter 4</u>: The Sealed Pharaohs' Tombs – Gadalla [Cosmology, Culture, Guide], Budge [Osiris I]

<u>Chapter 5</u>: Egyptian Temples of the Divine Forces

　　– The Function/Objective of the Temple – DeCenival, Gadalla [Harmony, Culture, Cosmology], Badawy, Choisy, Moessel, Pennick.

　　– Overall Conceptual Temple Layout – Gadalla [Culture, Harmony], Wilkinson RH [Temples]

　　– The Metaphysical Funnel Conduit Design – Gadalla [Culture, Harmony], Wilkinson RH [Temples]

　　– The Generative Significance of Jointing Patterns – DeCenival, Gadalla [Harmony, Culture, Cosmology], Badawy, Choisy, Moessel, Pennick, Gadalla [regular visits and being a civil/structural engineer]

– Outer Walls Physical/Metaphysical Protection – Gadalla [Culture, Harmony], Wilkinson RH [Temples]

– The Organic Foundation Roots of the Temple – Gadalla [Culture, Harmony], Wilkinson RH [Temples]

<u>Chapter 6</u>: **Architectural Constituent Forms of Metaphysical Functions**

– False doors – Aldred, James, Maspero, Wilkinson RH [Temples, Art], Wilkinson JG, Erman

– Recessed Walls – Gadalla [Pyramid, Historical], Wilkinson RH [Temples], James, Wilkinson JG, Erman

– Columns and Pillars – Gadalla [Pyramid, Historical], Wilkinson RH [Temples], Wilkinson JG, James, Wilkinson JG, Erman

– Capitals of Columns – Gadalla [Harmony, Historical], Wilkinson RH [Temples], James, Wilkinson JG, Erman

– Porticoes, and Peristyles – Gadalla [Harmony, Historical], Wilkinson [Temples], James, Wilkinson JG, Erman

– The Organic Colonnades – Gadalla [Harmony, Historical], Wilkinson [Temples], James, Wilkinson JG

– Obelisks – Gadalla [Historical], Wilkinson [Temples], James, Wilkinson JG, Erman

– Statuary Forms – Gadalla [Cosmology, Historical], Wilkinson [Temples], James, Wilkinson JG, Erman, Budge [Osiris]

– Roof Forms (flat, gable, corbelled, arch, & vaulted) – Badawy, DeCenival, Erman, James, J.G.Wilkinson, Gadalla [Harmony, Culture, Historical]

– **Giza Mastaba Tomb No. 6** – Reisner/Badawy

– **Other tombs during Old Kingdom** – Moessel [pgs. 22-23]

– **Khufu's Granite Room** – Badawy, Gadalla [Pyramid]

– **Pyramid Temple of Khafra** – Badawy, Gadalla [Pyramid, Culture]

– **Menkaura Pyramid** – Gadalla [Pyramid], Badawy

– **Peripteral Chapel of Sen-usert I at Karnak** – Badawy/ Lacan and Chevrier, 1946 [verified by Gadalla on location]

– **Wahka Tomb** – Badawy/Steckeweh, 1936

– **Karnak Temple** – Badawy/Chevrier, 1936, Gadalla [Harmony, Guide]

– **Osiris Temple at Abydos** – Badawy/Calverley, 1933 [verified by Gadalla on location]

– **Tomb of Ramses IV** – Pennick

– **Nectanebo II Temples** – Badawy/Ricke, 1960

– **Miscellaneous items** – Moessel [pgs 30-31]

– **Applications of Canon to Everything** – Moessel [pgs. 30-31]

– **Capitals of columns** – Badawy/Borchardt [1897/ Hölscher, Morgan]

– **Stelae** – Badawy/Lange & Schäfer [1902, Hölscher]

– **Pylons & Doorways** – Badawy/Hölscher, Moessel [pgs. 25-26], [verified by Gadalla on location]

<u>**Chapter 12**</u>**: The Animated Metaphysical Images** – Gadalla

[Cosmology, Culture, Harmony, Historical], Wilkinson [Temples], James, Wilkinson JG, Erman, Budge [Osiris], Piankoff, Badaway

Chapter13: Human Activities – Gadalla [Cosmology, Mystics], Wilkinson [Temples], James, Wilkinson JG, Erman, Budge [Osiris], Bleeeker, Piankoff

Appendix A: General Plans of Sample Egyptian Temples – Gadalla [Guide, Pyramid], Wilkinson [Temples]

Appendix B: Practical Mathematics in Ancient Egypt – Peet, Chase, DeCenival, Gadalla [Harmony, Culture], Erman, James, J.G.Wilkinson

Appendix C: Fraction Mysticism – Peet, Chase, DeCenival, Gadalla [Harmony, Culture], Erman, James, J.G.Wilkinson

Appendix D: Intentional "Irregularities" In Egyptian Works – Peet, Chase, DeCenival, Badawy, Gadalla [Harmony, Culture]

Appendix E: Monument Appropriations Reconsidered – Gadalla [Historical], Aldred

Appendix F: Sample Egyptian Sculpture Works – Gadalla [Historical], Aldred, Maspero, Wilkinson [Temples], James

Appendix G: Concrete Blocks Various Types – Gadalla [Harmony, Pyramid, Culture], Gadalla being a civil engineer

Appendix H: The Masonic Egyptian Roots – Gadalla [Harmony, Culture, Historical]

Appendix I: Egyptian Influence on Modern Architecture – Gadalla [Historical, Harmony, Culture]

Appendix J: Types and Forms of Mortals' Buildings – Wilkinson [all], Erman, Gadalla [Culture, Cosmology], James